MINISTRY WITHOUT MADNESS

MINISTRY WITHOUT MADNESS

Gordon Oliver

First published in Great Britain in 2012

Society for Promoting Christian Knowledge
36 Causton Street
London SW1P 4ST
www.spckpublishing.co.uk

British Library Cataloguing-in-Publication Data
A catalogue record for this book is available from the British Library

ISBN 978–0–281–06364–2
eBook ISBN 978–0–281–06849–4

Typeset by Graphicraft Ltd, Hong Kong
First printed in Great Britain by Ashford Colour Press
Subsequently digitally printed in Great Britain

To the people of
St John the Baptist Meopham
and
St Mildred Nurstead
for your fellowship in the
gospel of Christ

Contents

Foreword

This is the Gordon Oliver I know and admire and whose company I relish. It's all here – the warmth, the humanity, the godliness, the humour. Above all, this is a wise, searching book. It tells it as it is. This is ministry, in all its wonderful eccentricity.

I use the word 'eccentricity' deliberately. In ministry, we need to be 'off centre' (ex-centric), rather than colluding with the wisdom of the age. The danger is that pursuing this worldly wisdom may leave us only a step away from what Gordon calls 'madness', or from the various distortions of what it is to be a fallible human person with the most extraordinary task of carrying and commending the gospel of Jesus Christ. What Gordon Oliver does is to redirect our 'madness' into a form of godly humanity where we are neither as great as our publicity nor as flawed as our self-image.

'The only possible reason that justifies anybody being in ordained ministry', says Gordon, 'is that Jesus Christ is Lord, to the glory of God the Father.' The resurrection has given spectacular new meaning to what it is to be human, and it's this transformation of our understanding, both of ourselves and of those we meet in ministry, which keeps us alive, curious and committed. In the pages of this book (or the electronic version!) we meet a cast of wonderful characters, God's walking wounded, all looking for meaning or redemption or rest, or simply a way to survive.

But chief among the characters in the book is the person of the risen Christ, still wounded but glorious. And pointing unerringly towards him is another faithful character, the author of this wise, timely and compassionate book.

+John Pritchard

Preface
From certainty to confidence –
by way of stories

There are lots of books about how to *do stuff* in ministry. This is not one of them. Instead I want to explore how to live with the ministries God has called us to. I hope that readers who are not ordained will find the stories I tell and the reflections I offer helpful as they live their own faith journeys in fellowship with their ministers. Each chapter is built around stories and reflections from my own ministry. This is not because I think my experience is all that special, but because I think it reflects the normality of lots of ministry experience. All of the stories I tell here really did happen. In many cases I have altered the names and some of the details to respect the identities of the people concerned.

Being called to public ministry is all about being called to listen to stories, to take part in stories, to have stories told about you (some of them true!). Christian disciples are called to listen to the stories Jesus tells and to take part in them. We are called to be challenged, irritated, inspired and made to think again by the way other disciples of Jesus tell the same stories from their different perspectives and experiences. We are called to be part of the big story of God that we find told through the Bible and the lives of God's people before us, *at the same time as* being part of the small stories of God's presence or apparent absence when we listen to people in their homes, workplaces, down the pub, even in church. The main role of ordained ministers as people called to be publicly and locally holy and human is to tell the story of God at the same time as being called to live it with the wonderful, awkward and mysterious others we share our lives with.

'We trust in God – everybody else pays cash.' So says a sticker in a pub where I go for an occasional drink and a think after a hard day's ministry. It brings to mind another wry comment: 'I love God – it's his people I can't stand.' I find working in the Church enjoyable, maddening, inspiring, frustrating, exciting, depressing, absorbing, routine, funny, affirming and challenging. As a parish priest I work a lot with people who have rare and spasmodic contact with the Church at key turning points in their lives. Often they are openly curious about God and the faith stuff; sometimes they tell me that they are atheists (mostly I don't believe them); almost always they are people of goodwill who are keen to work with us; occasionally they are arrogant, aggressive, cynical, thoughtless and treat us like dirt.

I am welcomed into schools, community groups and work-places. Every day I spend time listening to and talking with God about the people he has given me to serve, and about what is going on in the world around us. Every week I lead the people in worship and praise and we open the Scriptures and celebrate the sacraments together. Sometimes our church is full to bursting with people who have come together for a good time. Lots of them know what it means to have faith and worship God and many others don't know the difference between being in church and being in any other venue. At other times the church is quieter – the people more attentive, reflective, prayerful, really open to God. My calling is to work with people whom God loves and has called me to love and serve too. I'm thrilled to bits that God has called me to be a priest – after all, what is there not to enjoy about it?

I arrived in my first ordained ministry post as curate of St John's Thorpe Edge, a Bradford council estate, clear about my faith in Christ, and clear that the people there needed the evangelical gospel I was going to preach and teach. Four gifts I brought with me stood me in good stead (though each has its downsides) and a fifth turned out to be a complete liability. First, I was curious – almost to the point of gormlessness. I have always been interested in what makes people tick, why they are like they are, what they enjoy, what they fear, how they speak or don't, what is happening and why. Second, I was open to noticing what was going on in people's lives – and often noticing the important bits among all the other things that were crying out for attention. Third, I was (and still am) completely useless at most things practical – I can break almost anything and cause any piece of equipment to malfunction just by being near it. I love music but can't play any instrument. I love art but can't draw or paint. I think communications and technology are vital aids to the gospel but I can't understand or operate them very well. This means that I can see a lot of what needs to be done, but I need other people around who can make it happen and I can't compete with them. Fourth, I was (and still am) open to learn from the people in the church and the community. I see myself as a learner and the people I work with as my teachers. This means – on a good day at least – that I am open to discover new directions in my faith journey and ministry.

The fifth 'gift' I brought was certainty. This was dangerous. I felt that it was vital to present myself as a confident minister with a strong personal faith who could preach and teach attractively and with real conviction, who could lead people to faith in Christ and who would soon learn how to manage a growing ministry team in a large church. To ensure this required certainty that the Bible provided the core teaching, the certainty that God was to be trusted, and the certainty that if we didn't know the answers we could soon find them. I still believe that we are called to attractive and effective preaching, teaching, evangelism, pastoral care and church leadership. But before many weeks passed I had made a dreadful, but life-giving, discovery. It was crystal clear that the people on the estate did not have the questions that matched my answers, and nor did I know where to look for the answers to the questions that they were asking. A famous preacher wrote in the margins of his sermon notes, 'argument weak, shout louder', and that is the approach I took. I thought that the difficulties I was having would ease up if I kept up the certainty, stayed confident and convincing, worked as hard as I could to get to know the people and prayed like stink.

Thank God it didn't work out like that at all. It didn't take long for the certainty, and the arrogance that goes with it, to erode as I found myself hearing the stories about what people were really living through. I soon found that certainty in ministry can easily shade over into pathology – even something like 'madness'. Something much more robust was needed, such as important basics about what it can mean to trust in the grace of God, to become quietly confident in Christ. This is not something you can grasp and hold on to. Archbishop Michael Ramsey remarked in a TV interview, 'God is like the soap in the bath – you've got him – and he's gone!' Certainty in ministry, as in other walks of life, can be manufactured out of our neuroses without our even noticing it; but quiet confidence in Christ comes as a gift of love that we receive when we stop making the noise that blocks out the sound of what God has to say. In ministry this gift often comes through the stories we find ourselves mixed up with.

If there's one principle about stories in Christian ministry it is this. Our first encounter with the story is always somewhere in the middle. We join in part-way through, hear it told, take part in it for a time and then move on, leaving the story to continue being told and lived by other people. This doesn't mean that we never see the fruit of our ministries, or never bring anything to completion. But it does mean that we have to be cautious about two things. First, we should be wary of the idea that we can become 'expert' in ministry in the sense of gaining mastery over it and bringing it under proper control. The idea that ministry is about power – intellectual, technical, psychological or even spiritual – can promote distorted theologies that lead to harmful religion. Certainly there will be times of great power at work in our ministries – but it is the power of God's grace, truth and love. Our calling is to 'prepare the way of the LORD, make straight in the desert a highway for our God' (Isaiah 40.3). Second, we need to be wary of the idea that 'we have done it'. As with all the best stories, in ministry there is always more to be discovered, more story to be lived and told.

Living through the middles of stories of people and communities means that there will be a premium on learning, listening, humility and mystery. We need to be perpetual learners, both of the big story of God and the local stories we are directly involved in. We need to let God make us good at listening – and that means not getting in the way of other people's stories. A friend of mine who was called to mediate between two violently opposed groups in a strike after a murder had taken place told me, 'I've been listening, listening, listening; I've been sweating with listening.' Because we live in the middles of stories we can't always be sure that we have heard the whole story, so we need the humility to be clear that we don't and probably can't know it all. This doesn't mean that we have nothing to say – nothing to contribute to the story. We certainly have, and that's why we are in ministry at all. But the priority will be on hearing the local and personal stories we encounter in the context of our living actively as characters in the big story of God.

One New Testament expression for what I have called 'the big story of God' is 'the kingdom of God'. Jesus taught us to pray, 'Your kingdom come, your will be done.' This means two things. First, the kingdom is shaped by Jesus – what he says, what he does, and above all by his cross and resurrection and his promised coming again. Second, it hasn't completely arrived yet. We live in the middle of the big and little stories of God, not just for the practical reason that we join in and leave part-way through the action, but for the theological reason that we are caught up in the coming of the kingdom of God that Jesus talked about. That's what being a Christian disciple and a Christian minister is all about. It is both mysterious and maddening. It is mysterious because although we can't see it all yet we live trusting that we will – in fact we stake our lives on that trust. It is maddening at times because the power scripts that are somewhere in all of us want to speed the process up and make it all happen sooner. This is not just about impatience or wanting to out-god God. We love God and God gives us love for people we live and work with. We want them to be set free from their suffering, their confusion, their childishness, their sinfulness, or whatever it is that is holding them back. Sometimes we think that if God got his divine finger out a bit sooner it would be better for everybody all round!

You can avoid the spiritual and emotional painfulness in ministry only if you can refuse the love of God and the love of the people you serve; just as you can avoid the pains of bereavement by hardening yourself against the costs of loving. But Christian discipleship and ministry are all about living with the love of God for the real world, or they are about nothing at all. When Jesus called his disciples to follow him in the way of the cross he wasn't joking, and he wasn't just using a useful metaphor for the costliness of ministry – he was expecting his disciples to follow where he was leading. Sure, the way of the cross of Jesus leads to resurrection and glory. As far as Jesus is concerned that's the only way that leads to resurrection and glory – the way of salvation.

I want to argue that although Christian discipleship and ministry can be stressful, painful and maddening, they need not drive us mad. That is why in the final chapter I focus on the importance of allowing our ministries to be demonstrations of foolishness. Foolishness comes more easily to some than to others. But we are all called to be 'fools for the sake of Christ' (Corinthians 4.10). Before I was ordained as a priest in 1973 I had to write an essay for the bishop. I titled it, 'Reflections of a Junior Fool for Christ's sake'. It came back with the title crossed out in red ink and the comment, 'a rather flippant idea – ordination as a priest should be taken much more seriously!' This flippant idea is the main theme of the rest of this book.

I need to say a big 'thank you' to all the people who have accepted my often bungling attempts at ministry and priesthood, and especially to those whose stories in one form or another appear in the pages that follow. Thank you also to those who have persuaded me to keep going when I wanted to give up – both in public ministry at times and in writing these chapters more recently. Steve and Vicky Coneys, good friends in ministry, and Anna Drew read the drafts and made useful comments and Mike Setter helped with the technical stuff. Alison Barr and the staff of SPCK have been more patient through the production process than I have deserved, and hugely encouraging. Thank you to my friend Bishop John Pritchard for taking the time from his incredibly busy ministry to provide the Foreword. Finally, thank you to my wife Ros, who has shared my whole journey of ministry so far, has witnessed all my lunacy and foolishness, and still walks the path beside me.

Gordon Oliver
The Rectory, Meopham

1

Called to belong . . . somewhere else

Just after I was ordained, my boss sent me to see an old lady in the parish. When I arrived she said, 'Oh, it's lovely to see you. Close your eyes and hold out your hands and see what God sends you.' I timidly held out my hands and she put something small and warm and wriggly into them. I opened my eyes to see that I was holding a baby hedgehog. Then she asked me to bless it.

If being in ordained ministry doesn't drive you mad it can drive you a long way in that direction! There are different kinds of madness, some of them madder than others. We can be madly in love, mad with joy, maddened by rage, or driven to despair. Our tastes and obsessions can lead other people to say that we are mad – about chocolate or jazz or pottery or quad biking or whatever. The pressures upon us can work with the pressures within us so that we become emotionally stressed out and our perceptions get distorted such that we become 'mad' to ourselves and those close to us. We may even succumb to mental illness and think of ourselves as 'going mad'.

These different ways of being 'mad' aren't necessarily all unhealthy – even our moments of rage and despair can mean that something within us is at last speaking the truth about how things are. The pressure to appear nice and kind to people all the time can lead to our developing habits of denying or suppressing the darker sides of our emotional lives. Most of the time we can find safe and healthy outlets for these 'dark powers' within us through our prayer lives, the acceptance and support of our families, and through our recreations. Lots of people in public life have to hold back some of what they think and feel if they are going to continue to serve well. These pressures are not unique to the clergy. But there are some things about being in ordained ministry that mean that we have to see things differently and to live differently from many of the people around us and even from some of the people in our churches. Ordained ministers are 'public Christians'. Our Christian faith, our sense of being called to our daily work by God rather than by the local council or the tyre factory, our commitments and our lifestyles can lead people to admire us and think that we are off the wall or a bit mad at the same time.

People often equate 'madness' with disturbance or illness. You are emotionally out of control, you've 'lost it', you can't see and respond to reality, you are 'in a world of your own', even a danger to yourself and other people. There can be an apparently sudden crisis (crises usually have stories behind them) or the build-up can be more drawn out and the period of 'madness' can last a long time. I know a bit about these kinds of 'madness' in my own experience. One day I was saying goodbye to people after a service and one of the men came at me yelling angrily and thumped me square in the face. When I went to see if he was all right a couple of hours later he told me that his son was being bullied at school and my sermon that morning about loving your enemies had, he said, 'made me so mad I couldn't help myself'. More long term for me is my own tendency towards depression – I call it 'having an available depression'. Twice in my ministry I have become depressed enough to need medication and take time off work to recover; I know that the possibility of becoming depressively ill is always there.

Readers will be worried about my linking the popular expression 'madness' with mental illness, so I want to say straightaway that the vast majority of people with mental health problems are far from 'mad'. We can leave visions of people raving in Bedlam out of our minds. But I want to stay with the word 'madness' in relation to ministry. This is because I believe that local congregations and institutional church structures can often be emotionally and mentally unhealthy places to live and work. They can be promoting and sustaining spiritual and emotional ill health at the same time as their daily talk is of 'grace', 'forgiveness', 'healing', 'fellowship', 'salvation'. Congregations where dysfunctional people exercise coercive emotional power over others and get away with it are commonplace. Parent–child dynamics between priest and people can make growing mature, responsible Christian disciples next door to impossible. Passive-aggressive resistance to change can make honest discussion and quality decision-making a rarity. Progress in church growth is made by inches if at all. And often this is how long-established congregations like it! This negativity is not the whole story, but we have to face up to these realities if ordained ministry is to be healthy and life-giving for both clergy and people. If we persistently ignore these realities we collude with the incipient 'madnesses' that give rise to them. We guarantee that the problems will remain and the mission of the Church will continue to be hamstrung. Here's a story.

For 40 years the congregation of St Ethelberger's has success-fully resisted every change proposed by a succession of incumbents. The wealthy congregation has halved in size through death, and the survivors have increased their giving to maintain things just as they are. The parish has a reputation of nursing a culture of selfishness and even of cruelty towards anybody who 'threatens' them with development and change. The Parish Profile, prepared as part of the search for a new vicar, contained glossy photos and the statement that, 'The parish is ready for change and develop-ment in accordance with our traditions.' Ten months after his arrival the new vicar went off work with a depressive illness. As he began to get better, his bishop suggested that he could receive some counselling before he returned to the parish.

Senior church leaders are short-sighted, and may even be negligent, if they sympathize with a priest who has had to stop work through stress but neglect to ask questions about all that could have con-tributed to the stress. These should include finding out about the contexts and structures within which this has happened. Whose stress and whose depression is the suffering priest actually bearing?

The 'madness' in ministry I am thinking of can take many forms. Here are just some of the ways they can show themselves. The minister may experience:

- an increasing sense of disintegration – feeling in pieces;
- distorted perceptions about reality – for example, about other people's motives;
- a sense of dislocation – being out of place;
- a fear of being misunderstood, unheard – feeling isolated without hope of relief;
- feeling demotivated – it's not worth trying to go forward, but nor have you the imagination or energy to get out;
- feeling overlooked or undervalued – left in the loneliness of not knowing how you are regarded by those with oversight.

There is something else too. This concerns the glorious madness of the cultures where we are called to live and preach the gospel. Within an hour of where I live there are dozens of theatres, hundreds of art galleries, thousands of restaurants and pubs; sports, cultural, entertainment and retail facilities unimagined by previous generations. London is 25 minutes away in one direction, Paris just over two hours in the other. Life is very good for lots of people – but not for everybody. Even apparently successful families often pay enormous costs, in the form of working hours as long as those of Victorian times, huge pressure to conform and perform, unremitting demands for compliance with assessment and appraisal schemes, and the effects of all these in their personal relationships.

From nursery school age onwards children are inculturated into the 'salvation by success' culture, so they learn to live under the kind of pressures they will experience when they reach adulthood. The miracle is that many appear to thrive on it all. The Church is well used to serving, praying and preaching in cultures of neediness, failure and sin, but how on earth are we supposed to serve, pray and preach where 'salvation by success' is the cultural norm? Christian ministers face the challenges of living and teaching the gospel of Christ that can seem like some kind of 'madness' to the world beyond the churches. And we do that with the ever-present awareness of our own neediness before God that can come from the painful gap between the message we preach and the way we really live. Are we Christians really so different? Or are we as caught up in the madnesses of our culture as everybody else?

Saved from madness by foolishness

My thesis is that the alternative to madness in ministry is not stolid, dull and boring versions of predictable religious 'sanity' (from which God preserve us!). Rather, I see the alternative to ministerial madness as the celebration of foolishness in the context of a clear and health-sustaining covenant. The right kinds of foolishness have the potential to save us from the wrong kinds of madness. That's rather an earful, so let me explain. I'll start with foolishness because that comes more naturally to me.

When St Paul preached, lots of people saw that what was on offer through Jesus gave a completely different way of looking at things and a whole new way of living. They wanted to be in on it so they turned to Christ. Other people thought that Paul was mad to talk so much rubbish. When he spoke at his trial in Jerusalem about the Messiah who suffered and rose from the dead, the judge told him, 'You are out of your mind, Paul! Too much learning is driving you insane!' (Acts 26.24). Paul stood his ground because he had learned (1 Corinthians 1.18ff.) that for those who can't see the point, the gospel of Christ crucified and risen from the dead *is* foolishness. Paul finds himself preaching out of the wisdom of God that gets heard as the best news in the world by people who aren't very powerful, not far up the social scale, and not always well educated. If the cost of preaching the wisdom of God is to be thought foolish, Paul will choose foolishness every time.

This foolish wisdom of God isn't just an accusation that Paul faces from Greek culture. Foolishness is the *essence* of the gospel. In the Magnificat Mary sings of her Saviour looking on her with favour, doing great things, scattering the proud, bringing down the powerful, lifting up the lowly, and feeding the hungry while the rich leave empty-handed. In his 'Jubilee Manifesto' (Luke 4.16ff.) Jesus stakes his claim as good news for the poor, release to captives, sight for the blind, liberation for the oppressed. In Matthew's Sermon on the Mount Jesus talks about having a righteousness greater than the Pharisees (the best of the best), loving your enemies, seeking God's kingdom first. Wonderful stuff! Great poetry! Inspiring! Yes, to all of that. But for Christians, including those in leadership, it isn't just wonderful stuff, great poetry, inspirational words. It is the life we are called to live, the economy we are called to live within, the ministry we are called to give our lives to.

This kind of foolishness puts us out of joint with the secular culture in lots of ways. It even puts us out of joint with some of what goes on in our churches. Unless we believe that the primary role of ordained ministers is just to be chaplains who bless congregations, we have to accept that this 'out of joint-ness' goes with the territory of being ordained. This does not mean that ministers have a licence to be socially naff, deliberately rude, self-seeking or living in their own little worlds. It does mean that we are called to live in ways that will sometimes make us marginal to the Church as well as marginal to society generally. If our ministries don't have that marginal edginess, at least some of the time, we probably aren't doing our jobs.

This foolishness can show itself in strange ways that, like all clowning, have a lot of ambiguity about them. One midnight I rehearsed for Spiderman's surprise visit to our church garden fête by walking in stocking feet along the ridge of my church roof to the point where I would dramatically announce my arrival – then stood there stuck and unable to turn round for a long time. The following day my Spiderman arrival went down big! Somebody said, 'We knew it were you in t'costume because of your belly! It's nice to see our vicar having fun with us – you don't seem so severe, now.'

My present parish has a farm shop where I sometimes go to serve at the butcher's counter, wearing my clerical collar and striped apron. People often ask what on earth I'm doing there. In another parish I sat in the darkness in a coal mine, waiting with a young man whose hand had just been severed in machinery. He asked, 'Why are you daft enough to come down this horrible place when you don't have to?' 'It's because you are somebody who really matters,' I told him.

Foolishness and covenant

How can we be sure that our foolish teaching and actions in ministry really are about the gospel rather than about what strange people we are? Often, of course, we cannot be sure. So what is it that can save our living out of the foolishness of God from shading off into eccentricity, or even stupidity? When Paul contrasts God's foolishness with human wisdom he is not just setting up two equally valid alternatives. He is talking about how God *chooses* to relate to people. Paul's theological roots are in the Hebrew Scriptures. This means that when he speaks about God *choosing* to do something, he is using covenant language. When you live in the covenant of God's choosing you know who you are, where you belong, what you are for and where you are going. In other words, you are clear what the deal is that God calls you to live with. Paul's linking of God's foolishness with the way that God chooses to get things done answers the question about why the foolishness we are called to in ministry is about living the good news of Christ, not about our personal or communal oddness. Paul says that when we are being true to the gospel, we are living with the wisdom of God – and that's something the world finds hard to take. But this is a central part of the deal – the covenant – we sign up to when we turn to follow Christ and when we accept the call to ordination. We will return to this in Chapter 8.

This provides a way in to the question of what kind of covenant there is between the churches and the clergy. Put more crudely, what are the clergy signing up to when we agree to be ordained? 'Covenant' expresses this relationship much more profoundly than 'contract' because it is rich enough to hold together relationships that include calling, freedom, loyalty, commitment and promise. In the covenant relationship with God described in the Bible, love, trust and freedom can flourish. Loyalty and faithfulness bring security; commitment persists through good times and bad; the promises of God are enjoyed in the present as foretastes of God's future. Now comparing the relationship between clergy and their churches to this kind of covenant could seem over-optimistic, to put it mildly. That is true, but for Christians all covenant thinking takes its character from the biblical understanding of covenant. Of course, there are different kinds of covenant in different settings. This means that we need to be clear about what the covenants that we take part in call on us to share, promise and deliver.

Until recent times the covenant between the Church of England and the clergy has been mostly implicit and assumed. The ordination service set out the shape of our ministry, the bishop's licence located it, the ground rules were provided by canon law and convention, and you got on with working it out for yourself. The raft of state and church legislation in recent years relating to terms and conditions of service, accountability and capability procedures, pensions legislation and lots more, make the 'covenant' between Church and clergy more clearly defined and explicit. It promotes a more contractual culture – at least at institutional level.

This more contractual clergy culture still leaves a lot of room to grow ministry relationships that will express gospel values in worship, learning, fellowship, practical service and other aspects of mission. What it does highlight, though, is the high value that churches place on capability and effectiveness as characteristics of their clergy. If they appoint clergy they expect them to perform. Priests can be fun. We can be holy. But we mustn't be fools. So where does that leave the gospel of vulnerability – the idea that God's 'foolish' first-choice option is often to work through people's weaknesses rather than through their power scripts?

I was talking to a doctor friend who made no secret of the fact that he was an atheist. In spite of this he had strong opinions about what kind of clergy the Church needs. He said, 'I don't think the clergy need to be very clever, or even to be particularly holy. But I do think that they need to be kind, and they also need to be human.' He spoke more wisely than perhaps he realized. What people appear to value most in their clergy are humanity and well-earthed holiness. Because we are rightly reticent about self-disclosure, it can be in moments of our unexpected vulnerability that people can most clearly see who we really are and perhaps also how we are with God. Most of us would prefer to lead in ministry with our power scripts rather than with our vulnerability – after all, much of what makes us vulnerable hurts; and we are all too aware of how open vulnerability – our own and other people's – is to exploitation. Times of vulnerability can be moments that provide doorways on to the grace of God for us and for other people. Here are two stories.

As a young and firmly entrenched evangelical cleric, I was used to seeing my parishioners in black and white categories. There were the 'spiritual' ones who came to the prayer and study groups I enjoyed running, and the ones who still needed to be converted who never came to prayer groups, but who ran the Christmas Fayre (God forgive me!). Olive was one of the Christmas Fayre people. A few days after our son was born, we were exhausted, stressed and didn't know where to turn for help. Olive arrived on the doorstep. She said, 'I know you don't think people like me are really Christians, but you need help and I've come to help you, so come on, let's see what needs to be done.' She brought love, comfort, a sense of safety, experience and a lot else besides. I learned that it was I who needed to be converted.

In my work as Bishop's Officer for Ministry and Training I gave everything I'd got to developing effective training and support structures for the clergy. I drove myself to exhaustion such that one day I sat at my desk and started to sob my heart out. I just

9

couldn't stop crying. My secretary Theresa wanted to call for help, but I couldn't bear the thought of anybody finding me in this state. At this point Bishop Brian stuck his head around the door in search of a cuppa. I felt embarrassed and ashamed. He waited until I was calm enough to hear what he had to say, then he said, 'Gordon, I want you to know that finding you like this doesn't make me think any less of you. You are my brother and you are suffering, so let's see what we need to do about it together.' I discovered that it was safe to be real about how I was experiencing my ministry at that time and that I could trust Brian to help me find my way through the crisis.

Clergy see local churches and the institutional Church at their best and at their worst. People welcome us into all parts of their lives; we get to see more of the corners and hidden places of people than almost anybody else; we get to rejoice with those who rejoice, weep with those who weep and wait and pray with those who suffer or wonder or wait. The greatest discovery I've made so far – it's perhaps early days yet, so I need the easiest lessons first – is that it's all about the love and grace of God that is sufficient for all our need because his strength is perfected in our weakness. Simple theology, but essential if we are to engage in ministry without madness that celebrates the foolishness of God in Jesus.

So far I have explored some of our own and other people's madnesses that we encounter as ordained ministers. I have said that the antidote to madness in ministry is accepting our calling to live with the foolishness of God in Christ. I have located this in the context of belonging as God's covenant people; and I have suggested that the gateway to God's grace for us and other people may be opened up through times of vulnerability as much as or more than through the exercise of our powers. This is all very well, but how might it work out when clergy have to face the practical realities of day-to-day ministry? I will start to explore this vital question by reflecting on the experiences of clergy going through transitions in ministry.

Setting out

Like becoming a Christian, getting ordained means saying 'yes' to the foolishness of God and investing absolutely everything that God gives you in that decision. It means 'crossing the line' and dealing with what happens when things change. Moving to a new ministry is like that too, so I set out on this journey towards ministry without madness by considering the kind of stuff that goes on when we move through transitions in ministry.

But to begin with, let's get three things straight. First, God calls us to ministry because he loves the world and he loves us. He wants us to fly free and enjoy his love and spread it around. God calls us because he loves us, not because he hates us, hates the world and can't stand the Church. This is something to get clear now, because a lot that happens in ordained ministry can draw thick clouds over this truth. Second, God knows how tough the world is and how wonderful it can be – and how evil too. That's why he comes to us in Jesus Christ. Our ministry starts with God in Jesus, not with the Church or even with us. Before we ever said 'yes', God said, 'I want you.' It's God's world. It's God's Church. It all has to be centred on God in Jesus. Third, the whole thing started with the resurrection of Jesus from the darkness of death. Our calling is to be witnesses with all God's people to the liveliness of the risen Christ. We can only do that in ways radically connected to the foolishness of God if we are wide open to the Holy Spirit giving us the oomph to get started, and to keep on believing and giving even when it hurts. Without these starting points there's no reason for the train to leave the station at all. Right then, with all this as basic, let's see what it can really be like.

Normally when you start a new job you turn up, find your workstation, the toilet, the coffee machine, the tool-store or photocopier, discover your first tasks and who you report to and get on with it. It's very different for new curates. Before their first day at work they have spent at least a couple of years in seminary, and they may have moved to new towns to live in houses that go

11

with the job. Their spouses may have given up their own jobs to make the move and the children left their closest friends and started at new schools. Before their ordination the new clergy will have gone into retreat to reflect quietly with God about what they were saying 'yes' to. At the ordination service the new curates wear their robes and clerical collars for the first time, the music is magnificent, the prayers solemn, the preaching (sometimes!) inspirational, the laying on of hands by the bishop deeply moving. Then there's a great big party – rather like a wedding reception. All very exciting for those being ordained, but it can also be challenging, both for them and for their families.

Jackie felt deeply disturbed by the sight of her husband Jeff, all robed up for his ordination, processing down the aisle: 'All I could see was it was just like a wedding – with him as the bride; and I wanted to shout out, "But he's already ****** well married to me!"'

A few weeks after I was ordained, I visited my family in Durham. Every night my dad would go to Neville's Cross Working Men's Club for his couple of pints. I went with him, still wearing my new clerical collar. After about an hour, as I played dominoes with him and his friends, he looked up and said, 'Well, that's all right then – you still belong with us.' He'd been worried sick that my 'becoming a vicar' would take me away from really belonging with the people I'd grown up among.

Elizabeth was ordained to serve as a self-supporting minister in the parish where she had already been worshipping for 15 years, while keeping her day job as a paramedic. She'd had lead roles in her church as home group leader, churchwarden and member of the worship band. As soon as she was ordained, she got the feeling that the people in the church didn't know quite how to relate to her now. They were still friendly enough, but they joked that they didn't know what to call her. They were having as much difficulty getting used to her in her new role as she was having herself.

Dave admitted that in the three months since his ordination his faith in Christ had started to become rather humdrum, routine, dull. Before, as a youth minister, he was really enthusiastic about sharing the faith in Christ that he found so fulfilling and exciting. He was fired up at the prospect of ordained ministry, but found it easier to talk about church and harder to talk about Jesus.

The move into first-time or to a new ministry brings experiences of 'crossing the line', whether the person is married or single and whether the move is into a new church as a paid minister or there is a change of role while staying in the same church. The physical, emotional and cultural transitions raise the question of what it is that we have said 'yes' to. It comes in different ways. Who do we belong to now? What are we for? What are we supposed to be doing? How do our public roles and personal lives fit together? What responsibilities do we have and where do they start and end? Where do we get the resources we need? Can we cope? Who can we trust? Do we really want to do all this stuff anyway?

This 'crossing the line' can be literally true. Before she was ordained Elizabeth would sit more or less in the same place in the congregation with her husband Jim and their friends. After she was ordained she was mostly robed at the front of the church, and Jim was still sitting where he usually did but without her beside him. This simple picture offers a kind of parable – ordained ministers and their families and friends are still part of the Church; but in ways that are sometimes clear, but often far from clear, they are now belonging to it differently.

If anything, the transition challenges get more complex as our ministries develop. When I was ordained, aged 24, all my belongings fitted into two small cases. I left college on Thursday, got married on Saturday, moved into our first house a couple of weeks later and was ordained soon after that. When I moved to my previous ministry post, at the age of 44, Ros was a consultant psychiatrist and had to find a new job, and our children were 15 and 11. It took two big vans and a horsebox to shift our stuff, and we had to rent out our house and start again in a new town nearly 200 miles from home.

Friends who have become bishops after being parish priests (there are some!) tell me that their biggest loss has been not having a local church they can really belong to with their families, where they can worship regularly and build up relationships they can enjoy and relax in. It takes time to adapt to the new context.

It isn't surprising that clergy, their families and church members can feel disoriented, confused and stressed at the same time as we experience the excitement of starting out on a new phase of our life and ministry. When we find ourselves in new territory it helps if we have a map so that we can get a sense of where we are and where we are headed. The one I offer here is my adaptation of the life-event transition theory first developed by Arnold van Gennep,[1] which is – or should be – familiar to every working minister (see the table below).

Life-event transition theory

Transitions and welcoming change Experiences and related work		
Separation *Agenda*	Transition *Agenda*	Incorporation *Agenda*
Parting	Making sense of	Learning to live
Bidding farewell	Tasks	with who you are now
Tearing	Resources	in the new country that God
Welcoming the	Identity	has called you to inhabit
challenge and	Purpose	with the new resources
the promise	Status	he shows you there
Owning reality and discovering hope that does not disappoint		

Separations

Jackie's experience at her husband's ordination service, mine in the club with my dad, Elizabeth now at the front of the church, and Dave with his worries about losing the 'edginess' of his faith, all show the power of the real and imagined separations that can come with surprising force to people in their first weeks and months of their new ministries. The phrase 'real and imagined' is important here. The physical separations are clear enough and comparatively easy to relate to, even if they can be stressful to live with. The inner confusions can be much harder to cope with, partly because we may experience them as feelings of general unease and partly because it can be easy to feel guilty about them.

Jackie had supported Jeff's vocation to ordained ministry from the start. They looked forward to the day when he would be ordained. They delighted in getting their new home how they wanted it. So when this odd thought about Jeff being like a bride came to her with such force she felt shocked. She didn't want to seem disloyal to Jeff by showing that she was disturbed about the changes they were both living through, so she tried to put it out of her mind – but in quiet moments she kept wondering what it was that they had said 'yes' to and how much they were leaving behind.

Jim smiled with pride when he first saw Elizabeth taking her place in the clergy stalls at the front of the church, but he noticed too that he felt a bit strange about it and wondered if they would ever again be able to worship together side by side as they had done for so many years.

Like many ordained ministers, Dave would say that he loved the Lord but wasn't so sure about the Church. As he sensed himself going off the boil spiritually during the first weeks in his new ministry, he began to wonder about what he was leaving behind as he crossed the line to take up his new role.

In this first phase – separation – there is a sense of being caught between two realities. The change we are living through is one that we have actively sought, vigorously prepared for and have been looking forward to. We welcome our new roles and look to God's grace and our new colleagues' support in finding the way ahead. At the same time we are leaving a lot behind. Some of it we are glad to see the back of; a lot of it, especially people we have come to love, we will miss. All clergy are volunteers, whether we are paid or self-supporting. We have agreed to our move, but that doesn't always stop it from feeling like a tearing experience. That's the reality of the separation phase – it involves a willing parting and a welcoming of what is new, but also a sense of loss and tearing as we leave behind some things that have been treasured – and it isn't always easy to tell which is which.

I left All Saints Huthwaite, where I had been the vicar, to start work at St John's College in Nottingham. Our new home was 14 miles from college, but for the first few months I used to make a 22-mile detour so that I could drive slowly through Huthwaite to see if I could spot anybody from the church. I didn't want to stop – it was just to know that they were there. This was part of my bereavement experience on leaving. After a while I didn't feel the need to do it any more.

Clergy can be so caught up with the excitement of our new ministry that we fail to notice the darker sides of the separation being suffered by other members of our family. Alan and Stephanie moved with their 11-year-old daughter, Carrie, to another part of the country to take up his new ministry. The move seemed to go well and they appeared to be enjoying their new home. Six weeks after the move, Alan and Stephanie were asked to see the head teacher of Carrie's school. They were shocked to hear that Carrie had been disruptive in class, took no interest in her lessons, and had been caught stealing from a fellow pupil. Carrie told them that she hated her new school, she hated their new house, she hated her dad's new job and she wanted to go back home to be with her friends again. She had tried, success-fully, to appear normal at home because Dad's job was about God so she had to pretend she was OK, but at school she just couldn't keep up the deception. Alan and Stephanie realized that Carrie was trying to cope with all the costs of all their separations all by herself.

The pulled-apartness of the separation phase and the need to give proper attention to what is going on for all members of our families can be masked by the drama of the ordination or the welcome service at our new church. The separation tasks include making a good parting, truly bidding farewell to what is ending, allowing yourself to experience the tearing, and welcoming the challenge and the promise of what is new. This is only the start of what we say 'yes' to when we accept the call to a new ministry – and all in response to the foolishness of God in Christ.

To reflect on and talk about

1 Look at the transitions diagram and consider: What changed for you and for other people during the transitions through ordination and the ministry changes you have experienced since then? What has helped and what has made the journey more challenging?

2 Do you recognize the pressure to achieve 'salvation by success' in the ministries you are involved in? What spiritual and practical resources work best for you in relating to such pressure?

3 Do you consider that 'foolishness' could be just a romantic fantasy or a genuinely viable ministry strategy for local church ministers?

4 What stories could you tell about people you know who you consider to have handled transitions in their ministries well?

2

Finding where you belong

———◆◆◆———

The TRIPS of transition

I have given the middle part of the journey the acronym TRIPS. Trips can mean journeys to new places but can also mean stumbling about, and that's what this main middle phase of transition is like. We find ourselves looking in three directions – back, around and forward. The looking back isn't necessarily just nostalgic or negative. None of us comes to our ministry 'brand new'. We arrive as the people we have become up to now and we draw on the experiences, skills and insights we have gained. Remembering and reminiscing can help us make connections, comparisons and contrasts that can clarify (or cloud!) what is going on in our new situation.

Memories are always partial, selective and nuanced, however committed we are to being truthful and authentic. We bring remembered experience into the present for particular purposes which may be conscious or subconscious, most likely both. Good remembering helps us place what is past in the past, locate ourselves truthfully in the present, and imagine new possibilities which will have connections to the past, but not be tied down by it.

As we reflect on our experiences as ministers in transition we have to discover how our faith, our imaginations and our fantasies relate to the realities we meet. Imagination, vision, fantasy and realistic engagement with how it will all play out are stimulated through reflection on our experience, prayer and conversations with colleagues, but still the transition into new ministry, where what has been experienced and learned has to be delivered, can be a very demanding and surprising one.

For 25 years I was a sector minister working in theological education and training, so I felt well equipped to take up my new role as a parish priest. In my previous two ministry posts I had prepared and led lots of worship events, most of them connected to conferences I was running, *but for 25 years I had not had to plan worship for the same community week by week for months at a time.* Here I was, the new rector with more than 35 years' experience, having to learn local church worship planning from scratch. How basic is that!

Tasks

First-time tasks in new ministries involve joining our new church (or our old church in a new role), and adapting to the whole range of roles, tasks, obligations and expectations. Most of us will bring useful experience and well-developed skills to at least some of this, but we have never done these things here before in the role we are playing now. It is disturbing to find that what worked well somewhere else doesn't have the same impact here. Questions crowd in and we may wonder if we can cope. Becoming sufficiently relaxed and confident to be able to worship God while leading other people in worship takes time. The first church I served in used lots of books – prayer books, hymn books, song books, pew sheets – and it seemed amazing that Jesus seemed to manage without such gubbins. I was learning to drive at the time. When the instructor told me to change gear, stick my hand out of the window and turn the corner, I didn't have enough hands. I found it like that learning to lead worship!

Many tasks of local church ministry are more or less highly visible – preaching, leading worship, working with groups, chairing meetings, praying with people. When we make mistakes people know it. They notice how we respond when things don't go as planned. Becoming appropriately confident and competent at the same time as being humble, committed and relaxed enough to apologize when we get it wrong and to keep learning are key values that we have to develop as we deal with what's in front of us. It can be a bit like trying to rebuild the bus at the same time as you are driving it. This does not always come easily.

As a new vicar I wanted to offer attractive preaching, teaching and worship-leading. Many people seemed to value my confident and clear approach, but others felt put down because they couldn't find it in themselves to believe and speak about their faith in the confident way that I did. One day, Margaret confronted me at the church door. 'You think we're a lot of hopeless hill-billies, don't you! You think we should all just believe and speak like you do. Well, you need to listen a bit harder, then you'll find things round here just aren't like that.' I felt devastated. I knew that she had seen through my façade of confidence into my insecurity, and that I should spend time listening to her, not to sort out her problems, but for her to help me to grow my ministry from more life-giving roots. I resolved that I would see my fellow church members, and later on my students, as my teachers. This is one of the few resolutions I have ever made that I have (nearly always) kept ever since.

That story is about taking proper time to really join the community we are called to serve and lead. It also raises the question of what systemic issues within our churches we need to get to grips with. Who holds what kinds of power and influence, how do they use it and what for? What hidden 'systems' are created by friendship and network groups that overlap between the church and the wider community? The baggage carried by these questions often gets unzipped when something has gone wrong, as roles and relationships start rubbing up against each other. A further important question concerns what opportunities and obligations come with our call to be clergy in our particular denomination, not just co-leaders of independent churches. A traditional way of describing this is 'taking holy orders'. I have written elsewhere that often clergy seem to believe that they have been ordained into a self-directed freelance ministry, so it comes as a surprise when they realize that taking holy orders involves *taking holy orders*! I will return to this area of discipline and discipleship in the last chapter.

Resources

Questions about relationships, roles and tasks naturally lead to questions about resources and support. Some local churches are rich in material, technical and administrative resources, but most are not. The greatest resource the local church has, apart from the grace of God, is people. Engaging with this reality can be a challenge in itself! It is very easy to preach from Matthew 10.2ff. that Jesus chose 12 very odd men to be his first disciples and they went out and changed the world. Having the godly love, vision, belief and practical engagement that will encourage Robert and Moira at St Muggin's to follow in the same way can be much more challenging.

Theological and other kinds of knowledge, communication and social skills, networking strategies and the human ability to gain people's personal allegiance, and more, are all part of the basic skill-sets clergy need. But in themselves they are not enough. Indeed, ministers who display the whole range of competencies to a high level can be a danger to themselves and to their churches! The congregation may grow (mostly through transfer from other churches) and the people think that their priest is wonderful. But the 'Christian spirituality' that is growing may be simply paralleling the ordinary human aspirations of the feeder communities. The people may actually be growing in a kind of conforming discipleship that has little to offer apart from the invitation to join a particular kind of friendship group (a church), rather than what David Augsburger has called 'dissident discipleship'.[2] Dissident discipleship commits people to live attractively for Christ in the world at the same time as challenging many of its unexamined practices and the values that give rise to them. For me and for most of the clergy I know, ministry practice that just grows a conforming discipleship is not enough. We are looking for ministry that bites much deeper into people's souls, attitudes and actions.

If the kingdom of God that Jesus called for could be organized into existence by church committees and mission projects, the job would have been completed long ago! However, the gospel we commend is not primarily about how we resource church-based processes, but how we live Christ-centred lives. St Paul writes to the faction-ridden church at Corinth, 'For the love of Christ urges us on ... From now on, therefore, we regard no one from a human point of view ... if anyone is in Christ, there is a new creation: everything old has passed away; see, everything has become new!' (2 Corinthians 5.14–17). It isn't compulsory to drive a wedge between the practices and processes of ministry and the love of Christ that urges us on to see people from a completely different point of view, but many of us end up doing just that.

This middle phase of the transition, with its two-way pull, gives plenty of opportunity to get our ministries out of perspective and to fall back into regarding everyone and everything 'from a human point of view'. The gospel begins to become old news to us. Our life of prayer becomes formalized or perfunctory. The faith that was so energizing before we were ordained becomes routine. For some it isn't long before ordained ministry, for all the fancy language and titles that go with it, becomes just another job that people do to serve their communities. Yes, clergy have real reverence for the teachings of people like Archbishop Michael Ramsey ('We are to be often with Jesus with the people in our hearts and often with the people with Jesus in our hearts'), and Henri Nouwen ('Here is the Father who ... has stretched out his arms in merciful blessing').[3] But our in-built self-esteem, acceptance and power scripts are so strong that these teachings are more often admired and romanticized than genuinely followed.

It is essential to get focused on the spiritual resources and gospel values that will energize and sustain us for this middle phase of transition at the same time as helping us to keep sufficient clarity of vision. The Church of England *Common Worship: Ordination Services* puts it sharply:

Deacons are ordained so that the people of God may be better equipped to make Christ known. Theirs is a life of visible

self-giving. Christ is the pattern of their calling and their commission; as he washed the feet of his disciples, so they must
wash the feet of others . . . Priests are ordained to lead God's
people in the offering of praise and the proclamation of the
gospel . . . They are to set the example of the Good Shepherd
always before them as the pattern of their calling.   (pp. 10, 32)

Soon after George was ordained, it was clear that his ministerial
skill-sets were underdeveloped in a whole range of key areas. His
domineering boss responded by subjecting him to withering
negative criticism and making him go on a series of courses – 'to
get yourself sorted out'. The only outcome was that George became
discouraged. His boss began to lose patience and he sent George
back to theological college, where I was asked to be his tutor.
On arrival he looked discouraged and depressed and said he
felt useless and wondered why he had ever got ordained. We
encouraged him to be open to God's love and God's call to love
the people, and to make that his priority. When he went back
to his parish, his boss gave him the job of looking after a failing
church plant in another part of the town, where he 'couldn't do
very much harm'.

The church plant was begun to serve a community of gifted
professional people. It met in the music room of a local school.
George knew that he could not compete with the highly developed
professional skills of his small congregation, and he decided to
put all his energy into praying for them and leading the worship
as well as he possibly could. He discovered which ones he might
encourage to work with him in the preaching and teaching. He
prioritized visiting people in their homes and workplaces, praying
with them and offering pastoral care in the form of faithful and
gentle friendship. He was now sure that God had called him to
ordained ministry, but confessed that he still couldn't think why.
He told me that he was not much good at anything – all he could
do in this new church was to love the people, discover what gifts
God had given them and try not to get in the way. Within a few

months the church plant had moved to a larger room in the school. Within a year it had moved into the very large sports hall. George's boss was mystified and wondered what the technique could be that worked so well. George explained that he didn't really know because all he seemed to be doing was loving the people, praying for them and making space for them to bring themselves and their gifts to Jesus. Unfortunately his boss was still mystified.

Clergy often preach that 'Jesus meets people where they are'. As we live through the often turbulent experiences of this middle transition phase, this is part of the gospel that we need to believe for ourselves. The greatest stresses, as well as the greatest opportunities, arise from the fact that we are human. The resources to strengthen and comfort us are delivered by the Holy Spirit coming to us again and again through the humanity of other people around us. My transition into my present ministry, just over a year ago as I write this, has been a rocky one, as I have made some basic mistakes. The two resources that have been most help have been my mentor (provided to new incumbents by the diocese) and my churchwardens, who have had the love and grace to be honest and patient with me and to pray with me.

Identity

Identity is the central word in TRIPS. This does not mean that our ministry is to be an exercise in self-expression worked out on the canvas of our local church and its people. It does mean that any major life transition we experience – and moving into a new ministry is certainly one of these – challenges our sense of identity.

Five basic expressions of clergy identity are: what we are called, what we wear, where we live and who with, what we do, and how we are regarded by 'significant others'. These feed into a sixth – who we experience ourselves as being. For most people most of the time these things are a bit like breathing – we just do it, we don't really think much about it. But carefully engaging with them can be important in making the person we are a doorway, rather than a barrier, for the gospel.

Clergy are given special titles – Reverend, Father, Vicar, Rector, Canon. People meeting us for the first time often ask, 'What should I call you?' We wear robes that signify that we represent something much more than just ourselves. Even if we don't wear robes, what we do wear will still be an indicator of who we think we are and how we want other people to see us. For most paid clergy our homes are 'tied houses'. We live among the people we serve, but the style of house and how we live, hospitably or otherwise, in it can carry its own messages. We do particular actions in leading worship, preaching, pastoral care. We serve people at gateway times of their lives – new birth, marriage, death. We listen, celebrate, bless, minister forgiveness, pray, teach . . . At such times our relationships with people can go very deep very quickly.

At the same time as so much is changing for us, most of our important personal identifiers stay the same. Alan is still Stephanie's husband and Carrie's father; I am still loved by Ros and persecuted by our cat; Dave is still crazy about retro heavy metal bands; Elizabeth is still a paramedic. When we move to any new place we take ourselves with us. This means that it matters how we understand who we are 'in ourselves' and what value we place on who we are.

It is a commonplace that many people in 'caring professions' value other people very highly but can have low personal self-esteem. In her study of the impact of parish ministry on clergy, Yvonne Warren comments:

> Ordination to the priesthood can provide not just a role but also a mask to hide behind. A person can feel set apart through the Episcopal laying on of hands at their ordination, and can hide their inner feelings of low self-esteem behind a 'godly' exterior. Such adults often seek leadership roles in order to attempt to restore their own self-image.[4]

Their determination to excel often arises from a drive to overcome their inner fear that their estimate of their inner selves will be justified if they fail in some way. In the middle phase of transition into a new ministry this can be played out in public as trying too hard to please people, being overly concerned about how well we are doing, being fretful and oversensitive to what people say, overworking and neglecting the need for rest; and in private by comfort-seeking strategies that at worst can be unhealthy and even addictive.

Two important ways to engage with one's low self-esteem scripts are to lighten up, and to get clear who we *really* are. As a lecturer I used to pray about my work, take great care to communicate as well as possible with my students and work hard to help them learn. One morning I was wallowing in self-regret because I thought that my teaching session had gone badly. 'I really don't know what God is trying to say to me right now – I feel such a . . . !' I confided to my colleague Ruth. She cut through the mood by saying straight back, 'I can tell you exactly what God is saying. He's saying, "I love you, you . . . !"' I will come back to the need to lighten up later, but first it is important to get clear who we really are.

St Paul repeatedly uses the expression 'in Christ' or 'in him' as his main description of a Christian. In Christ we have peace with God, are released from the power of sin, are set free not condemned, are beloved children of God, are heirs of hope and can never be separated from the love of God whatever happens (Romans 5—8). St John underlines Jesus' own teaching that he chose his disciples. They didn't choose him. We live to share God's good news, not because we happen to think that it might be a good idea or a sound career option, but because God called us and Jesus sent us. Christians understand that we are who God says we are, not just amalgams of our genetic, social and psychological inheritance. Christians are called to live out of the 'freedom of the children of God', not out of a sense of being restricted or trapped because of what has happened to us. In short, Christian disciples and Christian ministers are to understand ourselves to be agents, not victims. This could all seem self-indulgent, and it would be if it were not for the character of Christ who the Christian is 'in'. St Paul gives a healthy corrective when he calls on the church leaders and people of Philippi to 'look not to your own interests, but to the interests of others. Let the same mind be in you that was in Christ Jesus, who, though he was in the form of God, did not regard equality with God as something to be exploited' (Philippians 2.4–6).

This call to 'let the same mind be in you that was in Christ Jesus' should alert us to the likelihood that wherever we find ourselves on the transition journey, if we are being faithful to Christ there will often be a sense in which we don't fit in with everything in the surrounding culture. It is not just a matter of not having 'settled in' yet. This goes with the territory of being foolish enough to seek and work for the coming of the kingdom that Jesus lived and taught. You can avoid the discomfort that goes with this foolishness only by settling for a conforming ministry of unthreatening religious observance and blessing anything that comes in front of you. Otherwise, being thought foolish to believe and do what we believe and do is not optional. It can also have its lighter side!

The church gives opportunities for all sorts of human small-mindedness, lunacy and sheer comedy. In our cathedral the big services are meticulously planned, to the last phrase to be said, the last movement to be made. The orders of service for the leaders which contain the choreography directions for all this have in large letters on the front page, 'FOR INTERNAL USE ONLY'. I'd always wondered where to put all this stuff! At local church level I always find it a wonderful moment in a stiff and formal service when a child yells out that they are bored. They often speak for more than themselves.

Two big mistakes ministers make are taking the Church too seriously and not taking it seriously enough. Any intelligent person will see that making connections between Jesus as he is portrayed in the New Testament Gospels, the kingdom whose coming he announces and the visible Church of the twenty-first century

requires discernment, wisdom, insight, imagination, and sometimes an extraordinary sense of humour. My friend, the priest and
clown Roly Bain, calls this 'singing a strange song in the Lord's land'.
But that is what clergy are signing up to in accepting ordination
and persisting in public ministry. The lived claim of the present-
day churches is precisely that there *is* a vital connection between
who we are and what we do and the person, teaching and work
of Jesus Christ. Being faithful in Christian ministry involves being
faithful to Christ. It also means being supportive of the Church
and critical of it at the same time. A moment of dark comedy
for me (maybe I'm just a bit strange) came in a cathedral service
to celebrate the first centenary of the diocese. It was a cold, wet
evening, the heating had broken down, the sermon was dire, the
presentation candles wouldn't light and the organist ran out of
music while a great procession of bishops was shuffling down the
aisle. In the silence while more music was being sought, one
of the bishops reached up, took off his mitre and called out, 'Isn't
this appalling!' People laughed and clapped as the grim atmosphere
gave way to something like joyfulness and fun. We can look in all
sorts of places in our search for our true identity as clergy of this
all-too-human, half-godly (at best), unsatisfactory Church, but if
we look for this anywhere other than 'in Christ' we are looking in
the wrong place.

Purpose

Being in public ministry is a huge privilege. It can be joyful, fun,
stretching, ludicrous, and at times very tough as it takes us into
some of the darkest places in other people's lives and in our own.
When the pressure is on, being clear about why we are living and
working this way is essential to our physical, spiritual and mental
health. Our sense of purpose in ministry can be subtle and diffuse
rather than always as clear as we would like it to be. It is as much
felt as thought. It comes as much from our sense of belonging
and being 'in place' as from self-conscious reflection. It comes

from a sense of the rightness of our being clergy of our particular church, being at home in a particular 'tradition' within it, and belonging to a particular local community where we live and play. In most people's work, purpose and productivity go together. Some recently published Ministry Development Review schedules point firmly in this direction too, with a good deal of language about performance and effectiveness. I don't deny the importance of these things, but a Martha-like over-focus on them can risk diverting us from what is much more central.

Karl came to see me three weeks after his ordination. He told me that he felt guilty that he was not doing enough to justify his stipend. He had trained on a part-time course while staying in his job as night-shift production chaser at a pipe-works. As an activist he wondered if the quieter pace he was experiencing in ministry meant that he wasn't 'doing it right': 'I don't feel I'm producing enough ministry' (his actual words). Karl already knew that the call to ordained ministry is a call to be a particular kind of person, not just a call to do particular jobs for the Church, but he was just at the start of discovering how to live this way.

At the pipe-works Karl's purpose was to keep production up to speed. It didn't matter what kind of life he lived or person he was, provided that he was fit and competent for his job. Purpose in ministry is different. It has to be *discerned, discovered and practised.* True purpose in Christian ministry cannot be adequately described by expressions such as having vision, being knowledgeable and good at projects, possessing all-round competence – important though these can be. I am convinced that one of the most important qualities in a Christian minister is a habitual sense of curiosity – even a kind of gormlessness – which makes us keep asking what is going on, what God is calling for, and how to join in to help it bear fruit that will last. In ordained ministry, as in other things, it is easier to see clearly where you have been than where you are going. That is why true purpose in Christian ministry is so deeply rooted in praise, thankfulness and waiting – three key characteristics of true Christian prayer.

Embracing this principle, that purpose in ministry is primarily to be discerned, discovered and practised, can release clergy from being over-anxious to know where they are supposed to be going, and the pressure to project manage our churches into getting there as fast as possible. It carries permission to explore what it means to have a ministry of 'being' a particular kind of person in Christ for others. This ministry of 'being' may sound spiritually attractive, but it can also be very threatening and is open to being mis-understood. It certainly doesn't mean that the minister can skive while everybody else does the practical work. Not at all! It does mean that the actions of ministry will take place self-consciously in the context of God's love, God's call, God's self-giving in Jesus Christ and striving 'first for the kingdom of God and his right-eousness' (Matthew 6.33). Linking words like discernment and discovery to purpose means that the process is incomplete. In a sense it always will be. However conscious we are of God with us, there will still be times when we wonder what we are for.

Joan's husband Michael died suddenly on a Sunday afternoon, my birthday. I went round to their house as soon as I heard. The room was full of people sitting in silence, smoking, drinking tea. Nobody spoke. I sat down in a corner on the floor. I should be able to find something to say in the face of death, but no words came to me or anybody else. Just sighing. I felt upset at Michael's death, and angry with God for letting me sit there with nothing to say. After maybe 40 minutes I got up quietly, thanked them for having me and left, feeling curious, frustrated, useless. Late that evening Joan phoned: 'Thank you for coming, Gordon. We know it was hard for you, but we honestly don't know how we could have got through this evening without you being here with us. I don't know what it is, but it's not something you can bottle and sell, is it?'

Status

The age of social deference towards the clergy in Britain has long gone. Some people today do not recognize a priest even when we are wearing a dog collar. I was asked to take the funeral of a man in the village parish where I now work. When I went to see his family they invited me to sit down and started rummaging in a desk for some papers. They handed these to me and said that they'd had difficulty filling them in and hoped they were all right. They were insurance claim forms. I explained that I was the priest who would be taking the funeral service, not the man from the insurance company – as they say in some places, 'Close, but no cigar!'

The age of deference has gone, but churches are still too often status-ridden communities where people argue over who sits where, who takes precedence and why, and all manner of ecclesiastical trivia. As somebody observed, small ponds make middle-sized fish seem very big – at least to themselves. The argument I recently witnessed between two clergy about which of them should walk in which position in a procession 'on grounds of seniority' would have been familiar enough to the apostles James and John, but would have attracted a sharply focused parable or two from Jesus!

It is easy to see how all four of the other parts of TRIPS are important for a healthy sense of worth. Is what we do really worth doing? Are the resources we are using worth using this way? Is the life I am living as the minister worthwhile? Is what I am doing worth really giving my life to? These are all live questions for people living with transitions in ministry. Being able to answer them positively is essential to the minister's self-respect, freedom and confidence. What the pastoral psychologists call 'positive self-regard' makes it possible to leave behind self-defensiveness and be open and generous towards others. When somebody asked Jesus which was the greatest commandment, he repeated the most basic scriptural principle about relationships: the first commandment is that you shall love the Lord your God with all your heart and with all your mind and with all your strength; and the second is that you shall love your neighbour as your-self (Matthew 22.37–39). Being held in the love of God leads to a real sense of enjoying the freedom of the children of God and therefore freedom to love our neighbours – who, as Jesus goes on to show, can be some pretty surprising people.

Ephesians makes the connection between love, freedom and confidence explicit (3.16–17) in the prayer, 'that you may be strengthened in your inner being with power through his Spirit, and that Christ may dwell in your hearts through faith, as you are being rooted and grounded in love'. There is a world of difference between having well-rooted confidence in Christ and just being a Christian minister who is naturally assertive. There is a deep attractiveness in the faith of people who have a sense of quiet confidence and freedom that comes from deep within them because they have been nourished by being 'rooted and grounded' in God's love.

As we leave our former ministry contexts and allow them their proper place as we move forward into new ministries, we need to be kind enough to ourselves and our families (and parishioners!) to take time to make sense of these five aspects of TRIPS. For the sake of clarity, I have spelled out the main characteristics of each part separately, but of course they all belong together, there is lots of overlap and at times there can be more sense of chaos than of order. As we journey forward in response to God's and the Church's call we need to be kind enough to allow ourselves time to experience the different parts of the transition. They are not obstacles to overcome, but places where God can confirm his call and reveal more of his grace and love to those who are curious enough to be open to them.

Covenant and the call to belong

I have described taking up a new ministry as 'crossing the line'. You might protest that this only emphasizes an unhealthy division between the people and the clergy of the Church. It should be clear that this is not what I want to do. I do, however, want to emphasize that a whole number of things change when a person accepts ordination or moves to a new ministry. Some things are obvious. You don't get whole weekends off any more except for holidays. You have to lead worship whether you like it or not. Others are more subtle and I will explore them in the coming chapters. For the moment I want to highlight just one major change. This is the change in relationship – you could call it a reshaping of the covenant between Jeff, Elizabeth, Alan, Dave and their colleagues and the Church, both as public institution and as local congregation.

While they were still committed congregation members they experienced the Church mainly as a local worship, fellowship and friendship group. They probably also had some experience of the Church as institution. For example, all of them had served on their church council and as ministry team members; Jeff had been treasurer of his church, Alan had been the parish Children's Representative, Elizabeth had been a member of the Deanery and Diocesan Synods. Their levels of commitment were very high and they would not have thought of walking away, *but they could have.*

As soon as they offered for selection for ordination training they began to experience the Church as institution that could and would have a direct effect on their own and their families' lives. They engaged with the Criteria for Selection; they were asked whole sheaves of personal questions; they had to make decisions about where they would train and how their college costs and housing would be financed; they became aware of clergy appointments processes and of their obligations to their sponsoring bishop. Through all this and more they willingly submitted their sense of calling to scrutiny and began to see their personal freedoms and obligations in new ways. Often these processes were encouraging, at times inspiring, as possibilities opened up for ways of ministry they hadn't even known about before (Diana had never heard of military chaplaincy, but she eventually became an army chaplain). Sometimes, however, they experienced the processes as intrusive and even oppressive.

Through it all a major question comes into play which we have to face again and again throughout our life and work as the world we minister in changes, as the Church itself changes, and as we ourselves grow and change. It is this. Just what is supposed to be the relationship between the clergy and the Church that calls us into ordained ministries? Just what is the covenant between the Church and the clergy? What will it be like when the transition is over and we arrive at the place where we are meant to belong?

We have started working with these questions in our journey from separations and through the TRIPS of the transition. We have discovered that when we agree to be 'fools for Christ's sake' the covenant we live in is about the cultures, shapes, relationships and direction of travel of people moving forward because God is calling them to new places. Covenant is not a kind of more cuddly, friendly and 'Christian' version of contract – far from it! The life of the covenant community gets expressed when mercy and faithfulness kiss each other; when people forgive each other because they can't go anywhere together until they do; when they tell stories about where they have been and where they might be going; when they wonder how all this happened anyway and when they laugh and sing and cry and dance and walk quietly in each other's company. The covenant communities we live in have to be big enough, bold enough and inclusive enough to contain all this turbulence so that we can be set free to be truly foolish in our ministries rather than being driven completely mad. And this means that the clergy have to face up to what kind of people we are called to be. This is the topic for the next two chapters.

To reflect on and talk about

1 What would it take to promote 'dissident discipleship' in your local church?
2 Do clergy really 'cross the line' when they become ordained?
3 How do you experience your sense of who you are changing through your experience of public ministry?
4 What questions does George's story raise for you about ministry in your local church?

3

Called to be holy

———•◦•———

At the end of the thanksgiving prayer in the Eucharist I hold up the chalice and as we all join in words of praise to God, I can see a distorted reflection of myself in the silver, and God whispers to me, 'Always remember, Gordon, this is for you as well as for everybody else.' For me this is often a moment of tenderness, reassurance and renewal as I know again that God has called us to be holy people, and through Jesus has opened the way ahead for that to become a practical reality, not just a general idea.

The renewal of all-member ministry as the normal expectation in churches means that there is a lot of overlap between what clergy and lay people do. There are also lots of overlaps between what clergy and other community-based workers do. So what is distinctive about the clergy? We must be foolish enough to engage with this question if we are to be true to our calling. If we do not, it will be hard to avoid ministry that takes on an uncontrollable life of its own in which the sheer pressure of pastoral and organizational demands leads to busy, unfocused and ultimately exhausting activism.

As a curate serving in a down-market housing project parish I was desperate to be useful. I threw myself into practical helping of people and families in 'acts of mercy'. If they needed help with filling in forms, being taken to the housing department office, the hospital or the job centre, being tided over with money until their benefit cheque arrived, or somebody to sit with their ailing parent while they did the shopping, I was there at the centre of the action. Word got around that if help was needed Gordon would deliver it. I was a complete neurotic reverend liability. My training incumbent watched all this activity – for about six weeks. Eventually he said, 'Have you noticed something about this community? We have a wonderful police force, a marvellous social services department [he exaggerated!], an effective fire brigade, and a not bad bus service – and none of them is called Gordon Oliver. Now, it's wonderful that you love the people so much and you want to help them. A lot of them need a lot of help. But let's just stop and take stock, and think about who we are supposed to be and what we are supposed to be doing as ministers of the gospel here.' He had a lot more to say, and he said it with such love and care that I was able to hear it – well, most of it.

If we lose sight of who we are supposed to be (our identity), what we are supposed to be for (the values and commitments that energize us), and what we are supposed to be doing (the actions that integrate our identity, values, contexts and resources), we are well on the way to becoming disoriented and disillusioned. None of us will see all these things clearly all the time. But we are meant to see them clearly enough and often enough to direct and focus our ministries well. I know priests who readily admit to being 'busy, but bored' and who are becoming dispirited because they feel trapped in the routines of church and increasingly distanced from Jesus and his gospel that was the heartbeat of their call to ministry. They can no longer see the point of the way they are living and what they are doing, but nor can they find ways of stopping doing it for long enough to find renewal of their vision and spiritual energy.

Along with the rest of 'the priesthood of all believers', the clergy are called to be people of holiness. We are surrounded by holy things, work in holy places, might wear holy clothes, minister with people who use holy words, are commonly supposed to have holy thoughts. We preach holy Scripture and call the people to witness to the truth of the gospel through holy living and holy action. The thing that is most distinctive about the clergy is that we are supposed to be about God and the things of God. Our calling grew out of some kind of encounter with God in Christ that led us to the conviction, tested and recognized by the Church, that this was what we must spend our lives giving ourselves to. The details will be different for everybody. For some the call comes clear, insistent and urgent, as it did for me. For others it grows over time. But for all clergy the bottom line is that we are to be about God and the things of God; about knowing Jesus Christ and making him known; and about working together in the grace and strength of the Holy Spirit for the flourishing of people and communities in ways that reflect God's love, truth and justice – apart from that there's not much to it!

Ordained ministers are called to be *publicly and locally holy*. Clergy are public and visible representatives of the priesthood of all believers towards our churches and the people where we live and work. Unlike other community workers such as teachers, doctors and social workers, most clergy are required to live among the people they serve. Everybody can know who we are, where we live and what we are like to meet when we are on or off duty. This produces some of the biggest opportunities as well as some of the biggest challenges for local church clergy – that we are called to live as holy people publicly and locally all the time. The expectations this generates can be oppressive as well as liberating, for our families as well as for those of us who are ordained. I will explore this in Chapter 4, but first I will focus on five short Bible passages that make connections between the holiness of God and the calling of the people of God.

Isaiah 6.1–9

Isaiah tells how he was called to speak God's message. In the middle of worship in the Temple, with its rich ceremonial, music and art, 'I saw the Lord . . . high and lofty.' He hears the praises of God with the rolling cries of 'Holy, holy, holy . . .'. Faced with the blazing holiness of God, he sees himself as he really is and his people as they really are: 'Woe is me! I am lost, for I am a man of unclean lips, and I live among a people of unclean lips.' We could paraphrase this: 'I am living apart from the truth and my people have lost contact with the truth of how things really are.' Faced with God's holiness Isaiah is reduced to something close to despair, but however inadequate and unable he is to live and speak the truth, God is calling him. The angel flies and touches his lips with holy fire and declares, 'Your guilt has departed and your sin is blotted out.' Then the Lord speaks: 'Whom shall I send, and who will go for us?' And a chastened, forgiven and freed Isaiah says, 'Here am I; send me!'

The connection between God's holiness and Isaiah's calling is clear. There are strong hints here that the core issue that God calls Isaiah to face up to in himself and among his people is about living truthfully as the people of God. This renewal will only be possible when Isaiah faces up to the fact that he needs the touch of God's forgiveness if he is to have any hope of doing what God wants him to. There is a sense of surprise, unworthiness and submission about Isaiah as God calls him. He is probably taking part in Temple worship as he has done many times before, but this time it is different. God has something to show him and something to say. His sense of unworthiness is as plain as his vision of God is clear. 'Here am I; send me!' has far more to it than, 'OK, Lord, it's a fair cop!' Isaiah no longer has to fear that he is living a lie and is in danger of being exposed. He *is* a man of unclean lips; he *is* exposed to God's holiness. But the touch of the angel brings him cleansing not condemnation, healing not humiliation, release for God's work not restriction for his failures. The Lord has work that needs to be done and he has chosen Isaiah to do it.

Kate comes to see me one day. I've known her for a long time. Life has been very tough for her. She looks embarrassed, as if she's about to tell me some terrible secret. 'I know this is going to sound really crazy considering who I am and where I have been in my life,' she told me, 'but I think God might be calling me to be a priest.' Although she certainly has a colourful past, it doesn't sound crazy and it doesn't come as a surprise to me. I've been waiting for her to discover what I've been seeing in her for some time.

I know a priest called Charles who whenever he is leading worship, and often when he is preaching, seems to have a look of astonishment and curiosity on his face. He tells me that he never ceases to be amazed that God has called him of all people to be a priest.

Psalm 84.5–7

This passage is also set in the Temple. The psalmist sings with such delight at being able to spend time worshipping God that he even sees God's goodness in the sparrows nesting in the rafters and the people hanging around the doorways. 'Happy are those whose strength is in you, in whose heart are the highways to Zion', says straight out what holiness is about. Holiness is about where you are headed and the resources you need to get you there. Holiness is about calling, direction and gift. Having 'the highways to Zion' in your heart means having everything in you turned towards the worship and service of God who has called you. This can only come as grace and gift. Isaiah's vision and the pilgrim's song show them in their different ways coming 'into place' with God. There is a world of difference between being 'out of joint' and being 'in place'. If a person is 'in place' with God the work may be tough and the burdens heavy but progress *can* be made and there *is* a place to rest – and not just for the sparrows! People who are 'in place' with God can have a confidence that comes from knowing who they are, where they are headed and what they are for. For his weary disciples Jesus makes the connection between taking rest, renewing understanding, and working with the right resources (Matthew 11.29–30). He tells them: 'Take my yoke upon you, and learn from me; for I am gentle and humble in heart, and you will find rest for your souls. For my yoke is easy [fits you well], and my burden is light.' This describes the person who is learning what it means to be holy – really 'in place' with God. That's all very fine in the Bible, but to twenty-first-century ears it can all sound a bit super-spiritual, detached, unrealistic and even guilt-inducing. Can holiness be practical?

I was talking with some nuns who live by faith – no regular income beyond what is given to them. I wondered how this really works, and to be honest I felt a bit cynical about it. So I asked, 'What do you do if you run out of soap?' One of them smiled gently at such an obvious question. 'We just tell our heavenly Father that we need soap and he sends it.'

Leviticus 11.45

God's call, 'you shall be holy, for I am holy', in Leviticus, echoed in Jesus' call to his disciples to 'be perfect, therefore, as your heavenly Father is perfect' (Matthew 5.48), could also seem a bit detached and unrealistic. But if you look closely at the Leviticus 'holiness code' it doesn't take long to see that the holiness being called for is very down to earth and practical. The Leviticus passages talk about how you arrange your family life, how you treat servants and strangers, look after the interests of your neighbours, who you can and can't sleep with, how you care for the land and animals, identify priorities in community justice (sometimes strangely to twenty-first-century readers, to be sure), how you decide what your clothes will be made out of, what you should eat and what to avoid, how to protect women from exploitation, how to handle money, and limit the excesses of wealth and the misuse of personal power – and a whole lot more besides. This is what it means for God's people to live holy lives.

Simple, detailed application in Britain today of the whole range of Leviticus' expressions of what counts as holiness could easily get you arrested! Holiness means living up to date with God. Scripture has to be interpreted afresh and faithfully if we are to live holy lives today. The point is clear enough. God's call to be holy involves practical engagement with the world we live in, believing that it is God's world and that we are God's people in it. In describing the distinctive call of the clergy to be publicly and locally holy, I do not, of course, mean that the calling of lay people is to be only privately and invisibly holy! All God's people are called to live lives of practical holiness. Often we fear to do that because we think it will turn us into losers in a world that belongs to winners.

Jesus draws on the same tradition of practical holiness in the Sermon on the Mount. His call to 'be perfect, therefore, as your heavenly Father is perfect' comes as the punchline to sections of teaching about anger, adultery, swearing oaths, revenge and reconciliation, generosity in the face of unfairness, and loving your enemies – no detached spirituality here! The word translated 'perfect' is *teleios*. It carries the sense of completeness, even of wholeness. When we give way to unholy actions we do so out of a sense of incompleteness; we fear that we are losing out and must assert our rights, otherwise we will become victims, pushed around by other people. Jesus' call to be perfect (holy) is the call to become secure enough in our identity as God's people to be able to live generously towards family and neighbours; and even towards people who make themselves enemies. This is very different from the competitive 'dog eat dog' culture of winners and losers. Even imagining this as a practical possibility requires some kind of conversion in the way we see the world we live in and respond to the people we meet.

Steve is under pressure to get his sales figures up to target in the fire security company he works for. At weekends he enjoys running the church Youth Alpha course and he's thinking about training as a lay preacher. Steve is in every sense a highly committed and energetic Christian. He comes to tell me that he wants to stand down from Youth Alpha and to forget about preacher training because he just can't go on living a lie. The gap between the values he commends to the young people and the wheeling, dealing and half-truths he has to use to keep his sales figures up is just too great. He seriously wonders whether he can even really claim to be a Christian at all. Steve is wrestling with the impossibly(?) foolish call to live with holiness.

1 Peter 2.9–11

If you go around living out of generous love towards your neighbours and your enemy you risk being trampled over and ending up feeling like a nobody. Maybe, on the basis that Jesus called us to be wise as serpents, we ought to play the world on its own terms and simply be better at power games than others so that we can get God's work done more effectively. That is tempting but it is not the holy living that Jesus and the Scriptures call for. When the Church has been at its most successful in worldly terms it has often been at its most spiritually indistinct and ineffective in terms of living and commending the gospel.

The First Letter of Peter calls on Christians under pressure to find their security, identity, purpose, role and energy in closeness to Christ and faithfulness to their calling. 'Come to him, a living stone ... chosen and precious in God's sight, and like living stones, let yourselves be built into a spiritual house' (2.4–5). Their true identity is not described by their mockers and persecutors, but by their Lord: 'you are a chosen race, a royal priesthood, a holy nation, God's own people' (2.9). Their purpose and role are to 'proclaim the mighty acts of him who called you out of darkness into his marvellous light'. Their energy and resources come from the reality that they are people rediscovered, renewed, restored: 'Once you were not a people, but now you are God's people; once you had not received mercy, but now you have received mercy.' This is nothing less than a conversion in the way that they are to see themselves. This conversion is basic to what the Bible means by being called to holiness.

Steve's real struggle was with the sheer loneliness he experienced in trying to keep his real feelings about his workplace stress and his faith hidden, rather than be thought a failure at work, at home and at church. His relief, when he was able to have his story received with love, respect and acceptance and the offer to 'travel' with him in his struggles, was visible. His situation had not yet changed, but the place where he was seeing it all from had.

Romans 12.1–3

The most radical conversion needs to take place in our *faith imagination*. Most people we meet come to us in the middle of their stories. The problems they describe often have a long history that cannot in any case be undone. They feel that because of where they have been and what has happened to them, their present is constricted and their future options are closed off. They are condemned to live as victims of circumstance. Even when clergy would agree that 'Jesus meets people where they are', we may be inclined to agree with them that their situation is impossible. If they had been born to different parents, had different personalities and different opportunities things would have been different, but they weren't so they aren't. So we find ourselves listening again and again to the same stories and offering what comfort and encouragement we can while admitting to ourselves that nothing significant is likely to change. But seeing John or Sarah or Michael or Jeanette as people in Christ who are caught up in God's new creation project leads to the kind of thinking that is open to holy possibilities that come out of the conversion of our faith imagination. This is what liberates Christian pastoral practice from the recycling and reinterpretation of suffering and sets it on course towards the healing and the liberation.

In Romans 12.1–3 Paul makes the connection between what you do with your body and the transformation of your mind – the conversion of your faith imagination. Sometimes in ministry all we can do is place ourselves (our bodies) in the places where people are, encourage them to express what is really on their hearts, and wait to see what God has in his mind. My prayer when people come to me for spiritual direction is: 'Lord, help me to hold the door open and not get in the way.' Often this being present with a deep attentiveness to the person and to God is about all we can do. But in God's economy it is enough. The gift of holy presence makes enough space for God to open us up to new ways of seeing the present and new visions of what could be ahead. Mind you, the reality that gets opened up is God's version and can be mighty surprising. Twice in my ministry I have been approached by men in my churches who could not read or write and who told me they thought that now they had come to Christ he was calling them to be ordained. Knowing a lot about the way the Church of England's vocational discernment system works, and looking at these lively Christian men, so full of faith, my heart sank, but I still held the door open. I thought that the Church would make mincemeat of them. How wrong I was! Both of them grew in stature way beyond my own faith imagination as the Holy Spirit brought out gifts and graces within them. After long journeys both of them are today ministering very effectively as priests.

However, even with a converted (or, more likely, part-converted) faith imagination the clergy, like all Christians, have to face the tough question of what happens when the rhetoric about holiness and the realities we experience don't fit together. Being called to be publicly and locally holy can take us into very tough places, even in (especially in?) churches. Three stories of holiness being stretched and challenged show that this can happen in apparently trivial ways, in ways that threaten the well-being of a congregation, and in ways that have the potential to destroy people and communities.

We had a light-coloured carpet in our sitting room. One Sunday morning as I was getting ready for church I stood on a scarlet lipstick left on the floor by a young woman who lived with us, and skidded across the carpet leaving a vivid streak. I went ballistic and yelled at everybody in my family, then stormed off to church in a filthy temper (our lodger slept blissfully on). My sermon that morning had been written on the theme of repentance and forgiveness. My family were there in the congregation, but I had no opportunity to apologize to them for my behaviour before I started leading the service. The pulpit can be a lonely place at such a moment. That morning my distorted reflection in the silver chalice had special importance. There was urgent repair work to be done for all our sakes. Trivial events can take us into deep places where priorities must be examined, faith renewed, love restored, laughter shared again, joy refreshed – a small domestic journey towards holiness.

Howard was a churchwarden in his late sixties and a respected figure in the community. He had managed to keep quiet that he had spent eight years in prison in his twenties for the manslaughter of a young man in a street fight after he had been drinking heavily. Following his release he had moved to a new part of the country, got married, come to terms with his alcoholism, set up in business and raised his family. One day, when he was finding the struggle to stay dry more difficult than usual, he shared his story for the first time with another church member and asked him to pray with him for God's strength. The person he confided in sold the story to a newspaper. Howard and his family were devastated, the congregation were confused and the vicar found himself hearing a whole mass of opinions, accusations and stories. He asked himself if St Paul really meant it when he talked about looking at 'no one from a human point of view', and 'if anyone is in Christ, there is a new creation' (2 Corinthians 5.16, 17). The call to be publicly and locally holy is all about tough-minded, tender-hearted, costly engagement. If we are indeed to call people out of darkness into God's marvellous light we will have to come personally and spiritually close to folk who are experiencing the deepest darkness. In places like that it matters a lot that you know who you are, what you are for and who goes there with you.

In the 15 years that Andrea had been vicar of St Anne's she had led the church in numerical growth, redeveloped the buildings, started community projects and set its finances in secure order – or so everybody thought. It came as a tremendous blow to the people when Andrea was charged with fraud and suspended from her duties pending trial in the high court. I was asked to take the services in the church on the first Sunday after the news broke. What to say to this shocked and grieving congregation? In the middle of the Holy Communion prayer come the words, 'in the same night that he was betrayed . . .'[5] The message gently, lovingly and firmly delivered gave the call to bring the holiness of God in Jesus into contact with the sense of betrayal of the people. Gradually, over months, the congregation began to regain their spiritual and emotional strength and regain their bearings. Many of them were able to resist the temptation to rubbish everything that Andrea had done in her time with them. They testified to the fruitfulness of her ministry even in the face of what they now knew to be her flawed personal life. A large number of people told me how much they had loved Andrea and still did. If they had known how much she was struggling they would have tried to help her – gratitude, guilt, hope, worry, love? All of these no doubt, and more.

Is holy always good?

So far I have been exploring our call to be holy in terms of who we are called to be and what we are called to do – holiness in our character and our actions. I have assumed that 'holiness' is something good, something to be approved of, something to be reached out for. Surely this must be true if God calls us to be holy as he is holy. Yes – but it would be dangerous to assume that becoming more holy will make us more popular or even more effective as church leaders. Bishop Geoffrey Paul described the Church as 'a glorious ragbag of saints and fatheads'. Often it's hard to tell the difference, and most saints are a strange mixture of both! A brief reading of the lives of the great saints shows them to have been extraordinarily in tune with and transparent to God, but also often deeply flawed and very difficult to live with. Personally I feel almost as uneasy about defining anybody as a Saint with a capital 'S' as I do about defining somebody as evil. Such designations can project the best and worst possibilities of ourselves on to other people and avoid our having to take responsibility for how we are here and now before God. At best the 'big league saints' demonstrate that people can be publicly and locally holy at the same time as being people that God hasn't finished with yet.

That is not how 'saints' are seen in the popular media. Stories of holy people such as clergy who are caught 'at it' attract florid derision and hysterical condemnation in the red tops. Delight is taken in destroying people's reputations when their publicly holy personae are found to mask failures and inconsistencies. It is clearly right for clergy, as well as for anybody else who abuses trust, to be called to account, but it is also clear that there are people who seem to be just waiting for claims to holiness to be exposed as phoney. The unholy game of constructing other people as saints by making them into celebrities, then tearing them down from the pedestals where we have put them, enables even otherwise intelligent adults to live in a world of moral primary colours and avoid facing up to the many-shaded compromising realities of their own lives.

People are both attracted and repelled by imagined holiness. Mary Douglas titled her seminal study of people's behaviour in sacred places *Purity and Danger*. Huge numbers of people visit cathedrals, churches and other holy places and appreciate the sense of peace, stillness and spirituality that they find there, but they are cautious about going deeper by joining in the worship that is the sacred place's central purpose. This uneasiness shows itself in people's responses to the clergy and in the unease clergy sometimes have about identifying themselves publicly. Jenny was ordained to serve in the same church and community where she grew up. On her first Saturday after ordination she wore her clerical collar for the prayer meeting and when assisting at a wedding; but when she went to buy sausages at the butcher's shop she slipped it into her handbag because, without really knowing why, she felt uncomfortable wearing it in an ordinary setting. William's work as a priest often requires him to travel into central London by train. Conscious of the public profile of child sex abuse cases involving Catholic priests (he is an Anglican), he prefers not to wear his collar while using public transport. Wearing clerical dress or not is a superficial example of what it means to accept the designation of being publicly and locally holy. But the unease in evidence here indicates that people who are in 'holy orders' need to be able to live publicly and coherently with the ambiguities that come with the territory.

It can also have its lighter side. When I went to take motorbike lessons, the other students were all young lads. I had rushed to my first session from a service I had been taking. The instructor glared at the lads and shouted, 'Right you ******* lot, it's my ******* job to stop you ****** lot killing your ******* selves.' Then he turned to me and said politely, 'Would you mind just following me, Father?' Wonderful fun! Such stories abound. In many countries priests do not normally wear distinctive dress except when taking services. A French Catholic bishop once remarked to me that only three sorts of clergy in his diocese wore clerical collars – *les charismatiques, les neurotiques et les problematiques!*

Holiness is not something a person has achieved, and still less is it a natural characteristic – like some people are good at music. Rowan Williams puts it this way: 'Put the window in a particular place and the light comes through; put a person in a particular place and God comes through'; holy people 'simply tell you that the world is bigger ... So when I think of holy people, my first thought is of those who have made me see more'. Reflecting on the role of present-day 'saints', he comments:

> If ... a saint isn't simply an extra good person but a person who has learned how to live in a particular place so that the light comes through, we ought to expect most of the saints to be pretty uneven, not to say confused characters ... they are there to tell us that if we hang around in their company long enough, we may with them get a feeling for that other world where change happens not by effort but by absorbing love.[6]

The real challenge of being called to be publicly and locally holy comes from the fact that we are human. That is what we will explore next.

To reflect on and talk about

1 'Ordained ministers are called to be publicly and locally holy.' Do you think that being a Christian is really a viable option for local church ministers?

2 'Holy people simply tell you that the world is bigger . . .' What do you think it is about genuine holiness that can attract and repel people?

3 What do you think it could take to convert your faith imagination and that of the people in your church?

4 What helps you to keep ministering when you are under pressure and you don't want to?

4

Called to be human

Clergy are called to be publicly and locally human as well as holy. In the vestry block of the first church where I served as a curate there were three doors, labelled 'Ladies', 'Gentlemen', 'Clergy'! There is strong recent folk memory of the clergy being regarded as somehow a different species – a class set apart – from 'ordinary' people. In the past this dreadful misconception has been fostered by attitudes of the clergy themselves as well as by the people in and around the churches.

A few days after I was ordained as deacon I received a letter from my uncle Tom. This was an event in itself. Uncle Tom was a tough labourer and writing didn't come easily to him. If he was writing he had something important that he wanted to say. He told a story. It was about a bishop in the north of England who during the General Strike in 1926 wrote a letter to *The Times* complaining that coal miners were getting involved in philosophical political argument, whereas their proper place was working to win the coal by the sweat of their brows. His diocese was a coal-mining area and he hadn't bargained for the fact that some of the miners read *The Times*. A group of them lay in wait for him beside a bridge he had to cross to get to his cathedral. When he arrived they threw him over the side, 60 feet into the river. Fortunately for the bishop, the miners weren't too sure what he looked like and had thrown the wrong priest into the river. The victim survived with a soaking. At the end of his letter Uncle Tom said that he hoped I wouldn't get stuck up like most of the vicars he knew, because if I did . . .

If I had any inclination in that direction it was disabused in my first few weeks of public ministry. I have to wear a denture because my upper front teeth have never grown. One morning I realized halfway up the pulpit steps that I had forgotten to put my denture in. Pronouncing the words of the sermon while not opening my mouth too far was a nightmare. The congregation found it hilarious. After the service they told me, 'It goes to show that even you are just human, like we are.' What else did they expect me to be? And anyhow, what does it mean for the clergy to be human? Surely it means more than just doing something silly from time to time.

The Bible is full of stories about people God calls to get his work done. The fact that they are getting old or are very young, have a stack of personal problems, have messed up in life, been devious, lack confidence, can't put two words together without help, wonder whether God is really there at all – and sometimes aren't too sure that they want to get caught up in God's work anyway – makes no difference. If you tried to apply the nine or ten categories for selection for ordained ministry in the Church of England to the major characters in the Bible you would have a pretty thin time. But this only tells us that the people God calls today stand in a long line of needy sinners stretching back to Bible times. It says with St Paul that 'we have this treasure in clay jars' (2 Corinthians 4.7). It tells us that God could and did use earthy human beings then and encourages us to think that he can and does use earthy human beings now. But this still doesn't tell us what it means to be human, still less what it can mean for the clergy to be called to be publicly and locally human.

Being human can be defined biologically, philosophically, psychologically, sociologically, politically and in lots of other ways. These categories are sometimes called 'narratives' because they function as story-sets that try to get at what is distinctive or not about being human. Biology narratives understand human beings as an outcome of evolutionary processes and show how much we have in common with plants and other animals; sociology narratives tell stories about how human beings form interest groups and communities, develop idealisms and work together or compete to promote or subvert them or overcome adverse circumstances; political narratives explore how power dynamics and desired ideals operate and can be modified in the interests of particular groups. All of these narratives hold a lot of truth; but none of them goes much further than showing that human beings have evolved as socialized, consciously reflective animals that have the ability to make choices and decide to take actions in relation to each other and their environments. All of them describe the 'story' of what it means to be human from within – that is, people describing themselves on the basis of their inherited cultures, experiences, desires, capabilities, associations and relationships.

The Christian narrative makes a very different set of claims. Its core message is that you are not just what you or other people say you are, however learned they may be. The Christian claim about what it means to be human is that you are who God says you are. This shifts the ground of the discussion in a way that shuts off some dead ends and opens up new possibilities. The other narratives stake their claims in the ground of empirical observation, experiment and argument about what counts as evidence that you can use as a secure basis for action. The assumption behind them is that the only things that count are what you can see and what you can measure or assess in some way. By contrast, the Christian narrative makes a *faith claim*. This is a different kind of claim. It depends on the evidence of testimony. People who have experienced God at work speak and write about what they have seen and heard; and they show what these encounters with God mean to them and their communities. The faith claim that Christians make is based in the belief that God is as the Scriptures testify to him and that people today are caught up in the same economy and purposes of God as the people of the Bible were. We are part of the same community as Moses, David, Esther, Isaiah, Peter, Mary Magdalene and the rest of them. So we go back to our question. If God calls us to be human, what does that mean?

Created and called

'Who on earth do you think you are?' and 'What on earth do you think you are for?' are two of the most basic questions every thinking minister has to face. This is not about being self-obsessed. It is about how we will set about getting to grips with our ministries. The Bible's answer is that you are created 'in the image of God' (Genesis 1.27) and you will find your greatest fulfilment in your relationship with God and with the other people God has called you to love and live with and serve. As St Augustine prayed, 'You have made us for yourself and our hearts are restless until they find their rest in you.' The Bible story of the man being formed out of the dust of the ground and God breathing into him the breath of life holds together three vital truths about what it means to be truly human. First, it tells us that God made humanity to live in solidarity with the earth from which we are formed. Second, the transformation from the dusty form into the living being tells us that a person lives most truly when alive with the Spirit of God. Third, it tells us that being made 'in the image of God' means being alive to the self-giving love, energy, creativity and fruitfulness through community that are characteristic of God himself.

Genesis tells the comical story of God parading a lot of animals in front of the newly created man and asking him to choose one to be his helper and partner. The poor guy could count and name them (typical male attributes!) but just ends up confused and exhausted. The joy of his cry, 'This at last is bone of my bones and flesh of my flesh', shows that finally he sees who he really is because in the newly created woman he sees another person created fully 'in the image of God'. Watching the procession of animals has made clear to the man who he really isn't. He can't become one with any of them. The man and woman living with each other naked in God's garden testifies to their character as people made to find their true freedom, their true nature, 'in the image of God'.

Like everything else in these creation stories, the 'garden in Eden' has symbolic importance. The order and abundance, the river spreading its life-giving waters in all directions, the gift of a place to live and work and flourish – all stand in contrast to the shapeless chaos that is confronted, challenged and overcome by God as he calls out, 'Let there be light . . .' (Genesis 1.3). The menacing waters at the start of the story contrast with the fresh flowing rivers, teeming with life, that water the garden and make it burst into life. The garden with its tree of knowledge stands as the place where the man and woman truly belong (are truly 'in place') and have productive work to do. In theological language it is the place where the covenant between God and God's new created people really comes to life.

There is a strong view among Old Testament scholars that these opening parts of Genesis (and much of the rest of the Pentateuch) originated, or were edited into their present shape, during the exile of God's people in Babylon. That is, they were written to call the exiles to wake up and see their true identity, their true home and their true purpose as people loved, forgiven, healed and restored by God himself. Many of them had got used to believing the lie peddled by their captors that they were sub-humans, fit for nothing but unpaid toil, abandoned by their God whose Temple in their so-called promised land was laid waste in ruins. Some had realized that they had no way out of their present condition so they should just accept their lot and settle down as best they could. On this interpretation, the people who retell these creation stories for the first time are setting out to confront the exiles' hopeless acceptance of their half-alive sub-human existence. The storytellers and poets are determined to call the exiles to look again and see who they really are and what they are really for. It is no accident that Isaiah builds his liberation preaching for the exiles (Isaiah 40—42) so strongly around the creation and new creation themes. He is completely realistic as he faces their sense of hopelessness that they have got so used to that they can't see it any more. 'A voice says, "Cry out!" And I said, "What shall

I cry?" All people are grass' (what's the point?). Then a few lines later, the call to get real: 'Surely the people are grass. The grass withers, the flower fades; but the word of our God will stand for ever' (so) 'Get you up to a high mountain' and speak out. The message the Lord has for exiles (people out of place, living on scant resources, no more important than tufts of scorched grass) is that you are who God says you are. Human beings are created, called, renewed, liberated to live for God in the world with all its possibilities and its pains. This is the start of the Bible's version of what it means to be truly human. The exile doesn't put you beyond God's loving purposes. It puts you on the edge of discovering what they are. Here's a story.

I visited Lorraine in her home to interview her as a possible candidate for ordained ministry. Now in her forties, she has been almost blind since she was a teenager. She has a big personality, a lively Christian faith and a loud voice. People I interview usually want to tell me about their faith and Lorraine was no exception. But I want to find out about who people are 'when they are not being Christian', so to speak, because this will be one of the most important resources they bring to their ministries. Is there any more to them than being a church groupie? Lorraine told me that she likes to do 'a bit of woodwork'. In my patronizing way I imagined that this meant she might have made a toast rack or something like that. I asked her if she had made anything she could show me. She took me into her beautifully appointed kitchen, which she had just finished fitting out with oak-fronted units with carved roses on the doors. I asked her what she had found the most difficult part. 'Persuading my husband to let me use a circular saw,' she replied.

Lorraine told me that lots of people, seeing her with her white stick, assume that she is not very bright and is very restricted in what she can do. But for her there is no reason why her disability should mean that she has to settle for living like an exile. God has stuff for her to do and she plans to get on and do it. But there was another exile in that conversation. My vision needed to be released from the restriction that blinded me because at first I could see Lorraine's disability more clearly than I could see who she really is.

I see the Bible creation narratives as essentially stories and theology of *protest*. They protest against everything that treats people as sub-human; they stand against the notion that people should just settle for life that confines them and restricts their opportunities to be at their best; they stand against the idea that you are stuck with the present mediocrity and there is no way forward to anything better; they stand against the notion that if you have messed up with life you have no choice but to lay in the bed you have made for yourself because there is no way back. They stand against the idea that God has put you somewhere then abandoned you to get on with it. They are stories about human salvation – and human salvation is what the clergy and other leaders of God's Church are supposed to be all about.

St Barnabas' was a struggling and discouraged community church in the middle of an estate. A few people had been worshipping there since it was built in the 1960s. New people came sometimes but didn't stay very long. When the vicar left, the bishop asked me to assess the situation there and produce some recommendations. I reported that it was a failed parish church that should either be closed and the building sold, or could be linked with a neighbouring parish that could try to build it up again – send it into exile. To his credit the bishop rejected my recommendation and appointed a high-quality, very experienced priest as the new vicar. Within a couple of years St Barnabas' was on the way to becoming the thriving church it had been built to be. Faced with the depressing picture of failure, the bishop and his team decided to apply the theology of creative protest, and the result was, and is, a church virtually risen from the dead.

The first Genesis creation story says that after creating people, God blessed them, told them to be fruitful and to 'have dominion' (1.26) over the other living creatures (the misinterpretation of 'dominion' as 'domination' rather than care and stewardship is one of the tragic results of the 'fallen-ness' of humanity). In other words, God gives the people he has created work to do. These myth-stories provide ways into answering some of the main questions that burden and threaten to crush clergy and other people working in the toughest of places. Questions like, 'Who do you think you really are?' and, 'What do you think you are really supposed to be doing?' come straight out of this most basic biblical understanding of what it means to be human – created out of God's love in God's image; set free to share God's purposes. These points can sound so banal as to be hardly worth stating time and again. But in the face of the sometimes overwhelming pressures of personal circumstances and public ministry, including the relentlessness of the demands to be doing things that will make the church more visible and apparently effective, these foundation truths that our ministries are built on easily get hidden.

In his theological autobiography, Stanley Hauerwas[7] describes how, under the wearing emotional pressures of many years of marriage to Anne, who suffered severe mental illness before leaving him and committing suicide, and his work as a theologian, he frequently found himself living and thinking as if God does not exist. He describes himself as living at times as a 'functional atheist'. There are perhaps more clergy who share that actual sense of functional atheism than would care publicly to admit to it. At the same time as the pressures of ministry can work to make us lose touch with our essential humanity, we can also begin to slip out of the consciousness of being made 'in the image of God'. The two realities belong closely together. In my work as a spiritual director I often hear fellow clergy talking about their difficulties with awkward church members, or admitting to wondering why they were ordained at all. A question I find myself asking (and wondering about for myself!) is what would happen if we really lived as if we actually believed the gospel that we preach. What possibilities for dealing with the awkwardness in other people and in ourselves as clergy might open up from there? The awkward truth is that a lot of the clergy, for a lot of the time, live as if the gospel that we preach either isn't true at all, or is only really true for other people. This is one of the things that dehumanizes the practice of ministry.

The pressures of day-to-day ministry can expose us to saturation point with the realities of people behaving and living in ways that undermine our true humanity. It is worth highlighting just three types of these, though many more could be illustrated.

The first concerns our pastoral encounters with people. Clergy can find ourselves being with people whose suffering from the ravages of wasting diseases, abusive relationships, dishonesty and all manner of carelessness and sheer wickedness can be breathtaking. As I sit alongside a 30-year-old father of four small children in the last hours of his struggle for life, I just cannot pray without experiencing something of the pain, confusion and rage that I find in the psalms. When I am face to face with a woman who is sitting in her home next to her partner who has beaten her black and blue, I wonder how God can give me the wisdom, integrity, courage and faith imagination that will be needed to help them find the right way ahead. People who are determined to nurse hate-making grudges against their own family members or their neighbours for decades at a time can make us wonder whether the forgiveness and reconciliation that we stand for in Christ can be real or must stay in some realm of detached spirituality or disconnected piety.

The second group concerns the attitudes and actions of people in our churches. Like all priests, I have had to lead in prayer, preach, and minister the sacrament to people who have been bitterly angry with me, verbally abusive in ways that would have got them excluded from a doctor's surgery or a retail store, or disappointed with me because of something I have done or not done. This is part and parcel of public ministry (and it is far from being my dominant experience when leading worship!). But the emotional and spiritual pain can go deep, especially when the people who behave so offensively are key people in our churches who have shared with us in ministry, worship, hospitality and prayer. Among the gifts needed by local church ministers is the ability to keep on loving, welcoming and serving in the face of disappointments, put-downs and let-downs. We have literally to learn to live with forgiveness.

The third group concerns the difficulties we encounter within ourselves. 'Why do you want to be ordained?' a wise old bishop asked a young man. 'Because I have never had any doubts about my faith and I want to serve God', came the reply. 'Well, you go and find some doubts and then I'll ordain you!' grunted the bishop. Like everybody else in our churches, we have our own struggles and questions about faith. Jesus wouldn't have told his disciples to seek, ask and knock if he didn't expect them to have questions that needed answers, needs that had to be met, closed-off places that needed to be opened up. We are vulnerable as well as capable people who need the encouragement of affirmation; and we are sinners who need forgiveness. Like other people in public life, we sometimes make mistakes that are publicly visible. Too often clergy respond by trying to stand their ground even when it has gone from under them, being inappropriately self-assertive, or developing strategies of defensiveness that over time grow a culture of keeping people at arm's length. It can take grace and courage for us to admit that we are struggling.

A year ago Andrew became vicar of four parishes just outside a large town. Three of the churches were built centuries ago as private chapels to serve country houses, and the local gentry think that the duty of their priest is to do things the way they like to have them done. The fourth is a large church in an expanding village. Here the expectation is for informal charismatic ministry open to gifts of the Holy Spirit and with a strong emphasis on healing and deliverance ministries. Andrew had previously lived all his life in downtown areas of large cities and served his curacy in a dockside parish. He thought that he would like ministry in the countryside, felt truly called to his present ministry and was confident that God would lead him in equipping the people in all four churches for their gospel ministries. His three children have settled well into local schools and his wife Julie is enjoying her new job as a solicitor in town. Two months ago Andrew was feeling disoriented, disillusioned, depressed and trapped. The charismatic village church tells him that he is being too conservative and should 'follow the lead of the Spirit more'; the three manor churches have made it clear that they don't want any of the charismatic goings-on and there'll be trouble if Andrew tries to force them where they don't want to go. Andrew feels that he just doesn't understand the local cultures he is working within and doesn't have the gifts needed for ministry here. Two weeks ago the bishop came for a confirmation service and surprised and delighted Andrew by saying that he would like to come and spend the whole day in the parish to hear about his ministry and meet the candidates. Andrew decided to be honest with his bishop about how he was feeling. At the end of the visit the bishop told him that he was doing a wonderful job, laid his hands in blessing on Andrew's head and left. In despair Andrew called on a colleague. He started by saying, 'I don't know if I'm drifting or drowning. Julie says this ministry stuff is making me smaller and smaller as a person. I think if I don't get out I'll go mad, but I don't know where to turn. I tried to tell the bishop but all he did was to lay hands on me to press it all back down inside . . .'

When you are being dehumanized by your ministry, it may be true to affirm that you are not just who you or 'they' say you are. You are who God says you are. It may be true, but it is not enough. It still leaves us with the question of where we are supposed to find our humanity and get it renewed within us.

'In Christ'

St Paul uses the phrase 'in Christ' or 'in him' so often that it is almost a catchphrase that captures what it means for people to be caught up in the life of Jesus. Examples include Romans 8.1: 'There is therefore now no condemnation for those who are in Christ Jesus'; 2 Corinthians 5.17: 'So if anyone is in Christ, there is a new creation'; Galatians 3.28: 'There is no longer male and female; for all of you are one in Christ Jesus'; Ephesians 1.7: 'In him we have redemption through his blood.'

The Bible presents us with a procession of people behaving in inhuman ways and God still using them, but it also shows what it means to be as truly and fully human as God intended. This is what we see in Jesus Christ. As Dietrich Bonhoeffer preached, our calling is to become fully human even as Jesus Christ is fully human. Jesus shows us what it means to live in the image of God. I will highlight four ways in which Jesus demonstrates what it means to be human – incarnation, limitation, death and resurrection.

Incarnation

I found myself in an army barracks shortly before Christmas being required, with no notice, to take 'Chaplain's Hour' with a group of about 20 young soldiers a few days before their posting to an active war zone. They were anxious and I wanted to give them something about Jesus that could help them to know he was with them and for them. What to say to connect with these tough and vulnerable young men? I heard myself say, 'I want to tell you three things about Jesus Christ and then you tell me what you think: his mother Mary was probably in her early to mid teens when he was born; after Jesus she had another six children; they probably lived in a one-room house in a place called Nazareth.' One of them cracked a joke: 'Their house must have stank like our barrack room in the mornings!' Another looked as if he was remembering something: 'My sister had a baby when she was only 15. There was hell to pay when my dad found out she was expecting.' A third soldier said, 'Does that mean he wasn't posh? I always thought he must have been posh like the people at the church up our street.' We went on to talk through some of the feelings that they were having about their posting, about leaving their families at home, how they would be able to do their jobs, where they could look to for strength to get through. We looked behind the unconvincing Christmas kitsch and started to explore the hope that comes from God through the man Jesus Christ.

The Bible goes out of its way to put the humanity of Jesus in the context of the purposes and the glory of God. The birth narratives in Matthew and Luke bring together the earthy images of Joseph – confused, worried, not sure what to do; and Mary – visiting her pregnant relation Elizabeth, and then, nine months pregnant and away from home giving birth on the floor and putting her baby in a cattle trough; and the family fleeing as refugees with their baby to get away from the homicidal tyrant Herod. Matthew and Luke put these vivid human details alongside stories of dreams and angels, the hosts of heaven, magi following a guiding star, prophecies from old people in the Temple. These Gospel writers make no attempt to spell out a doctrine of the Incarnation (or of anything else). They simply tell their stories and leave their pictures of Jesus to do their work. Mark doesn't try to teach doctrine either. He misses out the birth narratives altogether. He simply launches in, 'The beginning of the good news of Jesus Christ, the Son of God' (1.1), then continues by placing Jesus locally: 'In those days Jesus came from Nazareth of Galilee and was baptized by John in the Jordan' (1.9). Then the story has the voice from heaven and the Holy Spirit coming on to Jesus in the form of a dove, then Jesus wrestling with the questions of who he is and what he is for, then straight back to the shorelines and streets of Galilee. And that is how Mark's Gospel proceeds from the start – theological claim, prophecy, heaven opened, and Jesus walking in ordinary places meeting ordinary people, all wrapped up together. John has had a lot longer to reflect on who Jesus is and what he is for. He opens with the deliberate echo of the first words of Genesis – 'In the beginning was the Word' (1.1) – and quickly moves into one of the nearest things the Gospels have to an explicit claim about the Incarnation: 'And the Word became flesh and lived among us, and we have seen his glory, the glory as of a father's only son, full of grace and truth' (1.14). From very early on, Christians have held that Jesus was and is God incarnate. The soldier who compared the morning smell of Jesus' home at Nazareth with the fug in his barrack room was closer to the truth than he might have realized.

Limitation

I sometimes think that it would be great if I could be in several different places at once – say, leading a quiet day on Franciscan prayer at the same time as doing a spot of fly-fishing 40 miles away, at the same time as conducting a wedding in the parish 20 miles yet further on. It would be great fun, but certainly no good for my ego. After all, I'm not God (a major piece of learning for every priest!). Being fully human means that we live with limitation. We live with the limitations of the growing and ageing of our bodies, the limitations of time and place, and the limitations imposed by our capabilities, personal histories and opportunities. We stretch our boundaries and find much more becoming possible than we might have dreamed of. But limitation is still a characteristic of what it means to be human, and this is as true of Jesus of Nazareth as of anybody else.

I used to hate my limitations. This started when I was a seminary student. My fellow students all seemed to be able to draw, play musical instruments, create drama, fix electronics – so they produced brilliant visual presentations, music and drama that could be used for street theatre, mission and evangelism. One of my own greatest gifts, I have discovered, is practical uselessness. I learned this after years of trying to be something I am not, sweating with tears on Saturday nights trying to produce visual displays for family services on Sunday mornings. The only talent I have ever discovered in myself is a constant enjoyment of being with people in all the light and shade of joy and suffering. A parishioner who I had been helping with a personal crisis enquired if she could do anything for the church. I asked her what she was good at. She was a children's book illustrator. A man whose child I was baptizing wanted to know if he could do anything to say thank you for the way we had welcomed his family. I asked him what he was good at. He played bass guitar . . .

But there is a difference. Jesus *chose* the limitations of being human. For everybody else, limitation is not normally a first-choice option. We can certainly choose to limit what we will say or do or be, to make space for other people. But just as often we see personal limitation as restrictive, something to be challenged. There is something subtle going on here. For many people the refusal to accept the restrictions that life has imposed on them – for example, through physical disabilities, poor early education, destructive relationships, dire poverty – can enable them to achieve wonderful things. For others, especially perhaps people who are naturally multiply talented or otherwise advantaged, the free expression of their full range of capabilities all the time could be discouraging and disabling, not to say exhausting, for other people. This highlights the importance of what the Gospels show about Jesus' willing acceptance of the limitations of his humanity. He wasn't playing at being human. He really was (and is) human.

The clearest statement in the New Testament about Jesus choosing his humanity (and one of the earliest) is in Philippians 2.5–11. Jesus, who has every right to claim equality with God, refuses to trade on that by standing on his rights, but 'emptied himself, taking the form of a slave, being born in human likeness. And being found in human form, he humbled himself . . . to the point of death . . . on a cross.' From this slave status of condemnation, God raises him up and shows him as he truly is: 'Jesus Christ is Lord, to the glory of God the Father.'

Here, who Jesus is and what he is for are caught up together. Earthy humanity in all its depth of limitation and the glory of God belong together because they are brought fully together in Jesus Christ.

Death

Like all other living things, we die. It might even be unique to human beings that we are able to reflect on our mortality. The death rate has always stayed the same for people – 100 per cent. The ecology of death is essential to who we are and how we live. Yet natural as death is to being human, in most cultures it has taken on all the symbolism of destruction, decay, evil and utter loss. Most people will do everything they can to avoid or delay death. As comedian Woody Allen quipped, 'I don't mind being dead; I just don't want to be there when it happens.' Particularly to be avoided is death without fulfilment or purpose – death as waste. The Gospels show Jesus as willingly giving himself over to cruel, unjust, wasteful death – the death of the person, as his Jewish contemporaries believed, cursed even by God. For the Gospel writers the incarnation of Jesus and his death belong together. They are both part of the salvation story not because someone is born and dies – where would be the news in that? – but because of *who* is born and *how* he dies. Christians have lots of different ways of interpreting what it means 'to be saved *through* the cross of Jesus Christ'. All Christians are agreed that the deepest and darkest dynamics of what it means to be human are plumbed by the loving self-giving that we find in the death of Jesus.

The first Christians began to make links between the teachings of the Hebrew prophets and the life and death of Jesus. As Acts 8.32–33 makes clear, this was happening very early on. By making the link with Isaiah 53.7–8, the first Christians showed their under-standing that in being crucified Jesus was not only taking on the full depths of what it means to be fully human; he was also taking on everything involved in a person who reflects the image of God being so physically, emotionally and spiritually destroyed as some-thing that has become sub-human. Jesus is emphatically challeng-ing and rejecting the cynical reducing of other people to being sub-human as he himself dies on the cross. Even as he bears the weight of the cursed, Jesus speaks: 'My God, why have you forsaken me?' (Matthew and Mark); 'Father, forgive them', 'Today you will be with me . . .', 'Father, into your hands . . .' (Luke); 'Woman, here is your son', 'It is finished' (John). The early Christians used the notion that as he died Jesus 'descended into hell' – 'he went and made a proclamation to the spirits in prison' (1 Peter 3.19) – to preach that even when people find themselves in hell Jesus Christ will be there for them because he still has something to say, even in hell.

I keep a supply of 'holding crosses' in my study – little olive-wood crosses with smoothed edges that people can hold on to when they need to know that God is holding on to them. Often if they are ill and too exhausted to say prayers, or when they are sitting for hours with a family member who is dying, people find deep comfort from holding on to this symbol of Jesus' closeness to people who suffer, are needy, are in pain, are coming to the end of their lives with us.

Resurrection

Incarnation, limitation and death are easy to recognize as part and parcel of being human, but what about resurrection? The reason why the books we call the New Testament were written at all is that the first Christians staked their lives on their conviction that soon after he was crucified Jesus rose from the dead. Without the resurrection there would be no Christian good news at all. Jesus of Nazareth would have no more significance today than, say, Socrates – probably less. St Paul was emphatic on this point: 'If Christ has not been raised, your faith is futile and you are still in your sins. Then those also who have died in Christ have perished. If for this life only we have hoped in Christ, we are of all people most to be pitied' (1 Corinthians 15.17–18). The reason we are in the gospel business at all is because of the resurrection of Jesus Christ. This isn't the place for an extensive exploration of the New Testament texts on the resurrection of Jesus. For this chapter about the call of the clergy to be publicly and locally human I want to briefly highlight five points: the risen Lord is the human Jesus; the resurrection is local; the resurrection is personal; the resurrection changes the whole story of what it means to be human; the resurrection sets the mission and ministry agenda. But first, a story.

'If it wasn't for the resurrection of Jesus I think I'd go mad!' Denis is vicar of St Monica's, an estate parish with high unemployment and high scores of deprivation on all main indices. His ministry is mainly with people whose lives are full of dead ends. The whole environment speaks of impossibility. Denis has lived and worked here for ten years so far. He loves the people and they love and trust him. 'We matter to God, us who live here. That means we matter. We have a lot of crucified people round here. Jesus' resurrection tells us that being crucified isn't all we are worth. It tells us we are worth more than that. When people start to hope they start to come alive. They start to see each other for the first time. They start to believe that they and their place can be different. They start to have respect. They start to do stuff that builds each other up. That's what I keep banging on about. We are here at St M's because Jesus knows what it means to be really crucified and because he's alive with us. That's what makes the difference. Without that I'd go completely mad.'

The risen Lord is the human Jesus

The incarnation, death and resurrection of Jesus are all one event as far as the Gospels are concerned. The first people to meet the risen Jesus were clear that it really was him. He was different in some ways – he could be there without their recognizing him at first, but it was definitely him, not some kind of ghost or apparition. Mary Magdalene meeting him at the garden tomb, the disciples in the upper room and 'doubting' Thomas were all clear about this. They had met the Lord. As soon as he spoke, Mary knew it was him. When he wished them God's peace, gave them his message and breathed over them in prayer, the disciples knew it was him. When Thomas saw him with his nail wounds, he knew it was him. That's where it started from. It matters who it was who died on the cross and it matters that it really is the same person who was raised from the dead. Without this the whole claim to have good news is just a load of religious mumbo-jumbo.

The quietness of the resurrection stories in the Gospels is remarkable. All of the main resurrection appearances in the Gospels take place in quiet, undemonstrative surroundings – a cemetery at dawn, a closed room, beside a lake, in conversation, on a journey, then over a simple meal. Angels only get walk-on parts. Heavenly hosts are conspicuous by their absence. Even after they have met the risen Jesus some of the disciples take a lot of convincing. The Gospel writers seem to go out of their way to downplay the drama of the resurrection. They want to emphasize that it is the human Jesus, the Christ of God, who has broken through the boundary of crucified death. The whole environment and culture of the people Denis serves as vicar of St Monica's shouts out messages about limitations so hard to overcome that it's hardly worth trying. The resurrection of Jesus is the opening page of a very different story about what it means to be human. Denis's calling is to teach out of the liberating truth of this story. That is why it is worth having a church there at all.

The resurrection is local

The Gospel resurrection stories all happen in places that you could go to and send an email home from. In and around Jerusalem, on the road to Emmaus village, on the shore of Galilee lake. They are as local as that. There is nothing ethereal or unreal about the stories – not even all that much that is very 'spiritual' – and they are presented as ordinary human encounters. There is very little by way of explanation of what it all means. The first disciples and the readers of their stories are left to work it out for themselves, with the guidance of God. This locality of the resurrection matters for our topic of the clergy called to being publicly and locally human. Part of the 'scandal' of the Christian gospel is that it is so embodied, so local, in many ways so ordinary – and, considering the huge emphasis today on spirituality – so 'unspiritual'. The message of the resurrection of Jesus speaks about what it means to be human from the locality where it first happened to the localities where all who receive the invitation and challenge of the gospel of Jesus live today.

The resurrection is personal

This is to state the blindingly obvious! The two stories in John where the risen Jesus deliberately uses the name of the person he is meeting make this point. Mary Magdalene recognizes Jesus when he says her name – perhaps in a special tone of voice that he used just for her. Presumably Jesus, being God, could have some choice about to whom he would make himself known in those first hours and days of the resurrection. So we must assume that his decision to have Mary Magdalene as the first person to meet him was deliberate. She may have been among the most personally needy of his disciples (though we don't know in what ways). The point is that the risen Jesus chooses her and gives her something to do – to go and tell the others. This story bursts with compassion and intention. It opens up a new chapter for her, and ultimately for the rest of the disciples. Whatever it meant for Mary Magdalene to be the person she was up to that point, it meant a whole lot more after she was included in the story of the risen Jesus.

John gives the story of Jesus meeting Peter beside the lake and renewing his call that Peter should lead the disciples from then on. Peter, who has three times denied Jesus, is given three opportunities to say again (and hear his own voice saying again) that he loves Jesus and will 'feed [his] sheep' (21.17). The way that John's Gospel presents the names is important, I think. The narrator uses 'Peter' – the nickname 'Rock' earlier given by Jesus – but he reports Jesus as using his friend's family name – 'Simon son of John'. In doing this the risen Jesus is taking Peter back to his roots, giving him back his past; and from there calling him again to his new role. This time the emphatic 'Follow me' is spoken to Peter by the risen Christ. The point is that Peter's panicked denial of Jesus had driven him into a fear-stricken sub-human version of himself. The risen Lord calls him again to embrace his new humanity. (Maybe that's why he gives him his name back too.) Here again we see opening up the first chapter of the new story. Mary Magdalene and Peter are called to see that they are not who their fears and failures say they are. They are who the risen Jesus says they are and they are for what the risen Jesus says they are for.

The resurrection changes what it means to be truly human

I said earlier that characteristics of ordinary humanity include those of imposed limitation and the boundary of death. St Paul describes the rising of Jesus as 'the first fruits of those who have died' (1 Corinthians 15.20). For Paul, the resurrection is not just something that happened to Jesus at a moment in history – though it certainly is that – it breaks the boundaries of living and dying for those Paul describes as being 'in Christ'. For the New Testament writers, the resurrection of Jesus redefines the whole agenda of what it means to be truly human in the economy of God. Paul sees the implications of this in relation to the major community dividers of his time (and ours) in terms of ethnicity, political/ economical status and gender relationships: 'As many of you as were baptized into Christ have clothed yourselves with Christ. There is no longer Jew or Greek, there is no longer slave or free, there is no longer male and female; for all of you are one in Christ Jesus' (Galatians 3.27–28).

Chris is the vicar of St Martin's, not far from St Monica's, also serving a large, outer urban estate parish. Chris is proud of his background of a fine public school education followed by service as an officer in the Royal Engineers. His curate was shocked to hear him complaining that the reason why St Martin's cannot attract enough people who are willing to serve on the church council is 'because the kind of people who live round here just aren't officer material'. With attitudes like that Chris was shooting himself and his ministry in both feet. His curate asked him whether he believed the gospel or not, especially the bits about Jesus meeting people where they are, accepting them and opening up new possibilities for them by including them in his resurrection community. Chris objected that the curate was being over-idealistic. The curate persisted with his question: 'If we just look at people as they are, even if we are right about how we see them, what's the point of us being here?' When fixed ideas about people's humanity and their capabilities are defined in this patronizing way by what they can't be expected to do, and when this comes up against the commitment to see them through the lens of the boundary-breaking resurrection of Jesus and his invitation to become a new humanity, there are bound to be tensions. For a start it has the makings of a rather stormy vicar–curate partnership.

The resurrection of Jesus sets the mission and ministry agenda

My spiritual director for many years was Brother Bernard, an immensely wise and mischievous Franciscan friar. He would listen with a gravely sympathetic look on his face as I poured out my sorry tale of ministerial woes and difficulties, raising his eyebrows from time to time, nodding sagely, accepting the whole story. It was by no means all self-pity. Much of my ministry was hugely challenging, stretching my imagination, experience, learning and faith to the limits. At the end of my story he would stay silent for a time. Then he would throw back his head and roar with laughter. 'Clever old God,' he would say. 'You've just described the most immense pile of shit. Now the Lord we believe in is the risen Christ. Let's see what he can do with a pile of shit like this. Come on. Let's discover what he has in mind for us.'

The only possible reason to my mind that justifies anybody being in ordained ministry at all, or that justifies the amount of time and human effort that goes into church organizations, councils and planning groups, is that 'Jesus Christ is Lord, to the glory of God the Father' (Philippians 2.11). This is what sets, or should set, the mission and ministry agenda for the local church and beyond. The resurrection of Jesus Christ redefines what it means to be truly human and to be called to live in the new economy of the coming of what Jesus called 'the kingdom of God'.

A friend of mine told me about a Christmas card he received. The front said, 'This Christmas act like God.' Inside it said, 'Become Human!' In this chapter and the previous one I have been calling us to take a major step away from the pathway to ministry with madness, by being foolish enough to actually believe the gospel we preach and to relearn some of the basic principles of our calling as priests to be publicly and locally holy and human. In the next chapter I will explore some of the practical realities that this theology has to be robust enough to resource.

To reflect on and talk about

1 What for you is involved in being called to be 'publicly and locally human'?
2 How far do you think the experience of exile is the context of your or of other people's public ministries?
3 Hauerwas described himself as living at times as a 'functional atheist'. What resonances does this have for you or for other ministers you know?
4 What questions does Andrew's story raise for you about the call to be publicly and locally holy and human?

5

Called to serve

St James' Parish Church was built more than 500 years ago next to the River Thames to serve the prosperous merchants, ships' captains and naval officers working out of the nearby docks. Their memorials are in all parts of this historic church. Today St Jim's is in the centre of a high-density housing area. The docks and many of the businesses closed long ago. The area has a run-down appearance and a generally 'up against it' atmosphere. Most of the small congregation of St Jim's have worshipped here for many years. They have seen vicars come and go and have worked hard to keep the place going, but maintaining a Grade 1 listed building and running a living church in a poor district at the same time is an uphill struggle. New people come into the church from time to time, stay a while, then drift away.

When Tim became vicar of St Jim's four years ago the people had great hopes. He brought a lively faith, a warm and friendly personality, huge compassion and commitment and lots of creative ideas for getting the worship renewed and the building opened up as a welcoming centre for everybody. The hopes have been justified, especially at Christmas and Easter when people have packed in to the special family-friendly services. Good links have been made with the schools and community organizations. The ministry of St Jim's is in better shape than it has been for years.

But it is all desperately hard and lonely work for Tim and even he is getting fed up. He is in ministry because he loves the Lord, wants to serve him and is committed to serving him here. He enjoys the community contacts and mostly finds the people outside the church refreshing to be with. It's the Christians in his church that he finds difficult. They depend on him to take the initiative in everything – even waiting for him to arrange church cleaning rotas, organize refreshments, make sure the heating is on, replace burnt-out lighting. They regularly turn up at his house on his day off to discuss some trivial matter that could easily wait for another time. To cap it all, they have an uncanny knack of asking his permission to do something or other at the most inconvenient moments. One Sunday Tim went into the church to get ready for the early service while a thunderstorm was raging. Water was pouring through the roof where thieves had stripped off the lead. While he was struggling with his outrage and with plastic buckets, one of the churchwardens asked if he should light the altar candles now or leave them unlit because there was still 20 minutes to go before the service. Tim gritted his teeth and told him politely what to do. A few days later he said to a friend, 'I'm fed up to the back teeth. It's just like dealing with a bunch of thick teenagers. They expect me to be their dad as well as their vicar. Why won't they just grow up?'

Tim's call to ordination came during a mission at the big suburban church where he came to faith and where he served as baptism team leader and member of the church council. When the bishop told him in the ordination service, 'Remember with thanksgiving that the treasure now entrusted to you is Christ's own flock . . . Serve them with joy, build them up in faith, and do all in your power to bring them to loving obedience to Christ',[8] he glowed with enthusiasm. Yes, the call to serve the people of God was the call he'd responded to. But after four years at St Jim's he's beginning to think he'd be able to serve the Lord better by going back to his old job in business management. At least there he would have a clear job description, decent working surroundings, congenial colleagues, personal privacy and the resources to do the job.

Most clergy, like Tim, respond to God's call to be servant leaders in the Church because they love God, love people and want to bring them together in worship, witness and service. They give themselves to all this with real dedication. When the balance between what is obviously 'ministry' – such as leading worship, preaching, pastoral care – and parish management tasks tips over consistently in the direction of management and maintenance, the frustration begins to build up. Clergy often say something like, 'I don't mind responding to Jesus' call to wash people's feet, but I do get brassed off when I have to listen (yet again) to people moaning about money, dustbins and drains.' All well-engaged ministry will have times of 'finding God in the ordinary', but where frustration keeps building and has nowhere to go it is only a short step from being frustrated with the Church to being disappointed with the God who called you. Clergy who are disappointed with God often find it hard to admit this even to ourselves. We are supposed to be in this job because God has called us and the Church has commissioned us. We are supposed to be able to cope because we are supposed to have faith and believe the gospel that we preach. So the feeling of frustration and disappointment may be denied or admitted only privately and held within oneself. Priests can begin to feel trapped – they have given up good jobs, disrupted their families, accepted low pay and tied houses. For what? To struggle endlessly with the sheer spiritual and emotional selfishness of parishioners who show little or no practical interest in joining in the mission of the gospel?

Who can the priest safely turn to for help? Fantasies that the bishop will think of us as low-grade clergy who can't cope if we ask for help can make even this basic step impossibly difficult. (In fact bishops welcome priests asking for help, are often excellent at making sure that we have the resources we need, and see clergy who are ready to face up to their negative pastoral and personal experiences as positive assets in their dioceses.) When this pattern persists, the ideal of willing service degenerates into drudgery. In my work as a training officer I often found myself asking parish clergy, 'We've talked about your training course. Now tell me, what's it *really* like ministering here?' 'Well, actually, it's like this', would come the reply, and the story of disappointment would begin to unfold. The opportunity to be safely honest opens new possibilities for hope that does not disappoint because it can lead to action that heals, renews and frees.

How then can the enthusiasm that motivated us to respond to the call to serve God by serving his Church be sustained and renewed in the face of pressures that can leave us disappointed with the Church, our roles within it and with God? I suggest that four resources are essential if our ministries are to flourish rather than fade – truth that sets free, love that heals, fellowship that holds, community that sends.

Truth that sets free

Christians use a lot of community-speak designed to promote a sense of belonging, caring, supporting: 'brothers and sisters', 'fellowship', 'working as one body', 'reconciling community', 'healing', 'forgiveness', 'new life in Christ', and so on. The Church *is* called to be the kind of community where people love one another, hold together in the fellowship, work together as the body of Christ, become reconciled after alienation, find healing and wholeness, and live – with – forgiveness. Granted that we are not in heaven we must admit that the delivery value of this language can be hard to see. Churches are like other local community groups where people fall out, compete rather than cooperate, put each other down, hold grudges. The difference is that, as we saw earlier, churches often use the language of personal and community transformation through the grace of the Holy Spirit at the same time as allowing these behaviours to persist unchallenged, often for decades. Far from being the gateway to freedom that it is meant to be, truth-telling in churches is often something that people fear. This is not just because we rightly value tactfulness and gentleness more than rudeness and aggression, but because we realize that the cost of facing tough issues can be higher in the short term than skirting around them.

For months Megan, the rector of St Julian's, had been arriving at church smelling strongly of mouthwash and body lotion. Her leading of services was becoming disorganized and her preaching (normally OK) seemed ill prepared. It was clear to her church-wardens and others that still, three years after her husband's sudden death, she was depressed and drinking heavily, but nobody felt able to challenge her about it for fear of causing offence. They loved their rector and felt that she was going through a bad patch of some sort and decided not to intrude into her grief. The problem went public when Megan failed to turn up at the crematorium to take a funeral. She had fallen asleep in her study after a heavy lunchtime session.

I used to start training team meetings by lighting a candle, saying a prayer, then beginning the agenda. One day, straight after I had lit the candle, one of my colleagues said, 'Before we go any further we've got something to say to you. Working with you is horrible. Your moods are making it really hard for us. You shut us out. We can't get near you. We want you to do something about it.' They were all ashen faced. It had taken a lot for them together to have the courage to be honest with me. Within myself I had been struggling for months, but had just tried to press on and hope things would get better. I knew they were right. I thanked them for having the love and concern to tell me, asked them to pray for me and told them that I would arrange straightaway to see my pastoral supervisor and my spiritual director (both of which I had been putting off doing). I adjourned the meeting so that I could be alone, then I picked up the phone . . .

If the Church really is no different from any other community group except for the language we use, we have ceased to be the Church in any meaningful sense at all. We are just another part of the community landscape. One of the four marks of the Church in the Creed is that it is 'holy', and this means that it must be committed to living truthfully. Only by facing the truth of who we are and what we are can we really take the first steps on the next part of the journey towards who God has called us to be. Jesus teaches that 'you will know the truth, and the truth will make you free' (John 8.32).

It can be liberating for clergy to have the opportunity in a safe and kind environment, such as a cell group, a counselling relationship, or good-quality spiritual direction, to say honestly how we really experience our ministries and what we would really like to say to God, given half a chance. Most churches are not the right settings for the clergy to be as open as this in public. But in the kind, committed, sustaining context where relationships can be depended on to be wholesome and trustworthy, truth and freedom can come together as the story is offered, received and held about how things really are.

Two resources that have been lifelines for me throughout my ministry have been my pastoral work supervisor, who helps me reflect on what my work brings to me and I to it, and my spiritual director, who accompanies me and challenges me in my Christian discipleship. They have been different people at different times over the years as circumstances and needs have changed, but I have been able to make sure that they are always there. I see both of them regularly, though (as we just saw) there have been times when I have been neglectful – usually when I needed them most!

Jesus taught that knowing the truth will set you free for a relationship with God that has no need for concealment, deception, denial (John 8.31–38). A little later in John's Gospel (14.6), Jesus makes two sets of connections that make clear why 'knowing the truth' is meant to be liberating rather than restricting for the people of God. In the first set he connects the truth with 'the way' and 'the life'. The English words 'the way' translate the Greek words *he hodos* – which to Jewish hearers gives the echo of the exodus, the great journey of liberation from slavery in Egypt to freedom in the 'Promised Land'. *Life* in John's Gospel is far more than being able to breathe, sit, read and chew gum all at once. Jesus means what happens when God breathes, raising up dusty forms that mean nothing much to anybody, into people who know that it's good to be alive because they are alive to God and each other.

The second set of connections Jesus makes with truth – and the one that changes all this from wishful thinking into practical reality – is with himself and with God the Father. He says, '*I am the way, and the truth, and the life. No one comes to the Father except through me.*' Jesus isn't saying three different things here. He is saying the same thing in three different ways. We can put it like this. To be called and commissioned by Jesus is to know the way – where you are going and what you are for; to be alive with Jesus is to raise your vision so that you see God as your Father; to live out of the truth in Jesus is to be set free to know God as the Father and released to live and work as the person and the priest he has called you to be. In Romans 8 Paul draws the contrast between a slave-like dogged existence dominated by fear, frustration and resentment and the spontaneous joy that celebrates who we really are at the same time as it can face the tough facts of life as it really is:

> For you did not receive a spirit of slavery to fall back into fear, but you have received a spirit of adoption. When we cry, 'Abba! Father!' it is that very Spirit bearing witness with our spirit that we are children of God, and if children, then heirs, heirs of God and joint heirs with Christ – if, in fact, we suffer with him so that we may also be glorified with him.
>
> (Romans 8.15–17)

When Tim describes his church people as 'a bunch of thick teenagers' who want him to be their dad he is expressing real pain and describing real people who he experiences as immature, selfish and dependent. Megan's parishioners, who have colluded not to approach her about her depression and the drinking she uses to escape from it, have a real problem – how to challenge the strategies and behaviours of a priest who can't find it within herself to face the truth about how she really is. They have seen her becoming diminished as a person and as their priest, but have been unable to do anything about it. There is no minimizing the difficulty of situations like these. But there is a deeper theological problem here too. Tim's parishioners have probably become like they are through decades of a church culture that allowed them to remain childish in their Christian faith. They have lost the ability to see who they really are as people of God (if they ever had it) so they have settled for a kind of spiritual infantilism that has made it impossible for them to grow up as people loved and liberated by the Holy Spirit of God.

Often in stories like these the truth only comes out when a crisis brings things to a head, so they can no longer be hidden and therefore be kept unavailable for God's forgiveness, healing and transformation. That is why crises in ministry, well handled, can be starting points of renewal. Of course, the deep truths within these two stories are likely to be very complex, but the central point remains. In both stories there has been a move away from understanding truth as a resource for liberation, and a regression to understanding truth as something that is difficult, dangerous and fearful.

If clergy are to keep on loving and serving when we are tired and hurting we need to rediscover the truth that sets free because it reconnects us to the life-sustaining love of God in Jesus Christ. This commitment to truth-living and truth-speaking is basic to the way clergy are to understand ourselves as people who are called to serve.

Love that heals

Clergy talk a lot about love, help people to realize that they are loved by God and engage in acts of practical loving service. Love is what calls us to keep on giving ourselves in serving other people. There can be three problems with this (among many others). Continually serving others can easily seduce you into the belief that you have life sorted. You have the power in yourself to help other people in their need. Second, you can become blind to your own need to allow yourself to be loved by God and other people. A kind of spiritual and emotional arthritis can establish itself within you without your noticing. Third, while giving oneself in loving service can be very satisfying, it can also be very tiring.

I'm told that I do a larger volume of one-to-one pastoral work than many clergy. For some reason people keep coming to see me to help them with their life journeys and their Christian pilgrimages. I've already said that I try to make sure that I see my spiritual director and my pastoral supervisor regularly. For a period I placed myself in psychotherapy because I wanted to explore how I myself could grow while I was helping other people without foisting my own personal agenda on to theirs. After an especially intensive week's ministry I was worn out. I lay down on the couch and said to my therapist, 'I wish I was a bricklayer.' As she listened in the silence that followed I said angrily, 'If I was a brickie I could lay thousands of bricks and go home and I wouldn't have to have a relationship with any of them!' 'You seem to be finding your caring crowding in on you,' suggested the therapist. 'Perhaps you wish you were not you . . .'

If we don't take time to reflect on our own power scripts, if we allow ourselves to remain blind to our own needs, if we neglect to attend to our own physical and spiritual health, we are building walls to defend ourselves from the opportunities, risks and costs of allowing ourselves to be loved. Yet being held in love is the most basic human need after feeding, shelter and safety. Without it the sense of self becomes distorted and the capacity to relate confidently to others – as others rather than as projections of ourselves – is restricted. Disconnecting the energy of godly love from the commitment to serving can lead to styles of ministry that are self-serving, manipulative and abusive – and all the more dangerous because ministers may be unconscious of our own deep motivations. This is why clergy, like any other Christians, need to be often opened afresh to the love that heals because it is the tough, kindly, strengthening love of God in Jesus Christ.

One day I got hopelessly lost on the way to a preaching engagement and arrived at the church 40 minutes after the service I was supposed to be leading was due to start. I felt embarrassed, angry, demoralized – certainly in no fit state to lead worship and preach the gospel. To my surprise the congregation were still there waiting. The churchwarden took one look at me and said, 'You must feel terrible. Come and let me make you a cup of tea while you have a moment to relax.' She explained to the congregation what had happened and that I needed some space so that I could properly arrive and be ready to lead them in worship. Then she came into the vestry, gave me some tea, and prayed with me for God's kindly grace and healing. Then, when I was ready, we began the service.

'Let love be genuine,' says Paul in Romans 12.9. He is talking about practical love that brings the resources to serve and keep on serving even when things seem well-nigh impossible. Genuine love – as distinct from the phoney or shallow kind – offers mutual affection, honour, enthusiasm, joyfulness, patience, persistent prayerfulness, generosity, hospitality. It is deep and strong enough to respond to cursing with blessing; to relate as well to people who weep as to those who rejoice; to refuse revenge in the face of insult; to feed those who make themselves our enemies; and to leave judgement in the hands of God. This is light years away from early twenty-first-century understandings of humanity as no more than a sophisticated version of animal life with love, however altruistic it may be, expressing no more than the disguised self-interest of individuals or their species. The kind of love Paul is talking about doesn't come naturally – as a sort of maturity of attitude that develops with experience. According to Paul it comes about through the transformation of minds that are set free to discern what God really wants of us, rather than being stuck in the ruts of conventional thinking (Romans 12.1–3).

This kind of love puts others first, but it does not do this by putting the self nowhere. Jesus' action of washing his disciples' feet right at the time when he is coming to the crisis of Gethsemane and the cross could not make this clearer. John makes direct connections between Jesus' self-consciousness, the depth of his love for his disciples and how he shows it:

> Jesus ... Having loved his own who were in the world,
> he loved them to the end ... Jesus, knowing that the Father
> had given all things into his hands, and that he had come
> from God and was going to God, got up from the table,
> took off his outer robe, and tied a towel around himself.
> Then he poured water into a basin and began to wash the
> disciples' feet.   (John 13.1, 3–5)

John is careful to give two details about what was going on. 'Jesus knew that his hour had come to depart from this world and go to the Father' (13.1). This action takes place at the threshold moment that all his life and work has been leading to. 'The devil had already put it into the heart of Judas ... to betray him' (13.2). Jesus washes the feet of his disciples (including Judas) in the context of the confusion and betrayal that is gathering before the final action of the cross. Jesus washes the disciples' feet because they need washing and to show them the connection between the love that they are called to share and the service they are called to give (13.12ff.).

I have often heard clergy preach about the love of God we are called to share, but I rarely hear them talk convincingly about where this might lead in terms of working together or making connections between ministry strategy and practical action. Instead we tend to talk about how authority, responsibility and resources might work. Most often these discussions lead nowhere because everybody is too busy taking care of their own patch. At national church level the debates about tough issues like how we are to relate to ecumenical partnerships, support one another with our financial resources, engage gender inclusiveness in ministry, commit to community action, often pay no more than lip-service to the idea that God's love might be the reason for considering these matters at all. Renewing the connection between love and service is vital for the refreshment of our ministry and the renewal of our witness.

There is a lot in ministry that can leave the clergy feeling emotionally and mentally bruised and worn out, as we saw in the examples given earlier. The way through this is the way of love, compassion, acceptance and kindness before it is the way of systemic strategies such as education, training, mentoring. The love that heals deals with the reality that bad things happen to good people. Far from seeing this as wasteful experience to be cancelled out and forgotten, the love that heals sees bad experiences as possible open doors for God's grace. My family name is Oliver, and it's true – I do want some more! I think God wants some more too. God is greedy to love and bless and heal and send. He isn't content just to heal what hurts and make it as if it never happened. God doesn't seem interested in making things unhappen. Rather, he seems to delight in making healed hurt a resource for the further blessing of other people.

Fellowship that holds

Jeremy has been vicar of three village churches for 15 years. He is a well-regarded pastor, though the country gentry in his parishes prefer to come to the traditional-style services and leave everything else to him because 'that's your job, Vicar'. Three years ago a new housing development began in the largest of the villages and so far the estate has grown to more than double the size of the original population. The development is expected to double again in size within the next five years. The diocese has offered Jeremy support and training in urban regeneration ministry, but no additional staff in spite of the hugely increased workload. The existing congregations are showing little inclination to welcome the newcomers or adapt their services to make them more accessible. Jeremy told me that he often feels very alone in his ministry. The other clergy in his deanery group are sympathetic, but don't seem interested in offering practical help and support. He finds it hard to see the connection between Jesus sending out his disciples in pairs and the Church's policy of requiring vicars to minister alone. He has seen a press report of an employee suing his company for workplace stress experienced through unrealistic workload and

unreasonable terms of service. He wonders whether he should sue
the diocese, if only to wake them up to the realities of how it feels
to be on your own in an apparently fruitless and unsupported
ministry. But he can't be bothered. He wonders where he can find
the help and encouragement he knows he needs.

Jeremy's experience is acute, but it is not all that unusual. The
sense of being on your own can be strong even where relationships
in the parish are good and ministry is apparently fruitful. Clergy
chapters very rarely provide the support that is needed – their
meetings are normally too brief, irregular and superficial to
provide the environment of 'holding in trust' that is needed. In
such circumstances the call to serve can begin to wear thin.

Cell groups of friends who commit to meeting regularly –
even a couple of days twice a year can be good – fellowship groups
and religious orders can prove effective strategies in encouraging
the human and spiritual flourishing of the clergy. A particularly
helpful group for me was the Jesus Caritas Fraternity. This
meets in small groups of clergy every month and every member
commits to praying for every other member every day. The
meetings begin with an hour of silent prayer, followed by an
hour of fellowship over a simple meal. Then the group spends an
hour on Bible study – normally the Gospel for the coming Sunday
(we've all got to preach on it!). This is followed by the hour of review
of life in which each person offers their review and receives comments from the others. The day ends with sharing the Eucharist
and prayer for one another. Group members pray and seek to live
in the spirit of the 'Prayer of Abandonment':

Father,
I abandon myself into your hands;
do with me what you will.
Whatever you may do, I thank you:
I am ready for all, I accept all.
Let only your will be done in me,
and in all your creatures –

I wish no more than this, O Lord.
Into your hands I commend my soul:
I offer it to you with all the love of my heart,
for I love you, Lord, and so need to give myself,
to surrender myself into your hands without reserve,
and with boundless confidence,
for you are my Father.   (Brother Charles de Foucauld)

The high level of commitment to one another in prayer, meeting, fellowship and worship builds a community of deep trust where experience can be safely and truthfully shared, cherished ideas, hobby horses and recycling of grievances challenged, and roads to reconciliation opened up.

This level of commitment would be too much for many, but the point is clear enough. For many of us the 'essential supplies' of love, fun, grace, truth and freedom that can keep us fit enough to follow the call to serve can be found by clergy genuinely joining our own churches (as distinct from just working in them) and finding good-quality fellowship there. But there can also be real blessing from having access to a supportive group of colleagues who know what it is like to be in ordained ministry and who can provide the quality of fellowship that not only holds to account, but holds together with the love of God in Christ.

The New Testament teaching about unity and diversity being held together with the bonds of love in the body of Christ (1 Corinthians 12—14) is meant to have delivery value. The effectiveness of our mission and the sustainability of our ministry depend on this being transferred from the rhetoric of our teaching to the reality of our living. Christians in the traditional churches of Britain have got so used to talking about the amount of resources we haven't got that it has become an almost unquestioned part of our church cultures. The reality is that we have huge resources that are squandered by the failure to engage the most basic gospel values of the fellowship that can hold unity with diversity together. The way to resolve this impasse is through repentance that enables the clergy and the Church to come to a new mind about how to conceive of our ministry and mission; and in the quality of fellowship that has the capacity to hold together the realities of who we are and what we are working with.

Community that sends . . . and that welcomes

When Church of England bishops license new ministers they make a statement about community: 'Receive this charge which is both mine and yours.' The truth that frees, the love that heals and the fellowship that holds are core values of community that is genuinely Christian. This quality of community has the capacity to look beyond its own survival needs and take the risk of sending out its best people to live, demonstrate and teach the gospel message. This being rooted in the community of the people of God and being sent out from it is what makes being ordained as a Christian minister different from going out and getting a job. We see this dynamic of belonging and sending right through the Bible from Abraham to the sons of Zebedee. A person or group is open enough to hear the call of God, rooted enough to belong within the community of God' people, and sent out to serve the purposes of God. Jesus calls his disciples into community with him so that they can watch and listen, learn and practise, be inspired and challenged, before he sends them out to 'make disciples of all nations' (Matthew 28.19). Paul is sent out with others to preach the good news (though there is more than a hint that the Jerusalem church found him too hot to handle!).

Ministers today, like the first generations of Christian preachers, place high value on their connection with the community that sends them. This connection is what legitimates our ministry. We do not work on our own behalf. We are not self-appointed Christian leaders. We are people who are accountable because we 'submit to one another out of love for Christ'. Self-appointed and self-directed ministers often achieve popularity (or notoriety), establish their own churches, and have a strong tendency to recreate the gospel of Christ in their own image and for their own purposes. This kind of freelance ministry can certainly give people what they want – often at a price. But without the accountability and resources for spiritual renewal and pastoral care and discipline that are found in the best of Christian community, they are open to charges of self-serving and even of abuse.

But wait a moment! Where the structures of clergy ministry are allowed to become so loose as to be virtually meaningless, such as when formal commitments to minister in partnership with one another under the leadership of the bishop are routinely disregarded both by clergy and their leaders, the reality comes uncomfortably close to the kind of freelance self-appointed ministries I referred to in the last paragraph. That is why the communities that deploy, support and sustain ministries need to have ways of holding their people accountable for the content of their teaching, the wholesomeness of their example, the holiness of their lives, the quality of the care and service they offer. The disciplines and structures of ministry are there to help this to happen.

A useful question to ask is, 'Would you want to belong to this church if you were not its vicar?' My own answer to this is definitely 'yes'. I love the people and churches I serve. I find friendship and fellowship, and thoroughly enjoy living here – though we do have our moments! But for some of my colleagues the extent to which they and their families join their own churches can be a bigger challenge. Ursula was recently appointed as vicar of All Souls, a run-down parish in an inner urban area. The local comprehensive school was in 'special measures' at the time they were moving into the parish, though it seems to be improving under new leadership. Where will Ursula and Jim's children go to school? Where will they mainly do their shopping? What leisure facilities will they use? Their children will be the only young people in their church – there hasn't been a children's group there for years. Community that sends and that welcomes is about practical questions like these, not just about wide-ranging principles, however important they may be.

Another question concerns what the call to serve actually means in relation to community that sends and that welcomes. Church profiles prepared for the appointment process often use such words as, 'We are ready for an exciting period of change under the leadership of our new vicar.' But when change is proposed it doesn't take long to discover that readiness to change depends on which direction and over what timescale. The reality may be that the congregation are ready for change – as long as it doesn't make any difference.

Clergy have two roles in local churches that have to be held in creative tension. Through prayer, worship-leading, teaching and pastoral care our role is to help our churches to be *stable and well-rooted enough for them to flourish and grow.* At the same time we may have to challenge the established patterns and practices of our churches so that they become *unstable enough to move and change* as we engage with new questions, opportunities and challenges. The tension between these is inevitable. If we are to 'proclaim the Gospel afresh in each generation' we will need the graces and gifts of the Holy Spirit to keep the tension creative. The leadership we are called to give can be even more challenging than the service we are called to offer. This is where our journey takes us next.

To reflect on and talk about

1 How might truth-speaking in churches connect with the call to holiness and freedom?
2 What stories can you tell about 'love that heals' people in Christian ministry?
3 What questions does Tim's story raise for you about the relationship between ministers and congregations?
4 'Would you want to belong to this church if you were not its vicar?' What issues does this question raise for you or for ministers you know?

6

Called to lead

———◆◆◆———

Wanted: Incumbent with good pastoral and interpersonal skills

Most churches advertising for a new vicar put leadership in mission high up in their priorities, so Maureen was especially attracted by the advert for a new rector for St Martin's. St Martin's said that they were seeking 'a new incumbent with good pastoral and interpersonal skills who will relate well to people of all ages and help us move forward together in our mission'. She loved being a pastor and enjoyed her first six months in post as she took time to get to know people, threw herself into parish events, joined St Martin's Singers, and showed real effectiveness in leading well-planned Sunday worship and giving excellent pastoral care through funeral ministry. The trickle of complaints about her ministry was small at first – just a few negative comments here and there – but soon the trickle started to flow stronger. She began to pick up comments that she was spending too much time with the choir and didn't seem interested in the youth work; she seemed to devote a lot of time to the pastoral care team, but didn't seem very interested in the buildings group; when people argued about the hall rental charges she didn't seem too fussed one way or the other; church council meetings were argumentative and she didn't seem to be in control.

Maureen began to hear more and more about Canon King, her predecessor. People whose views she had come to respect told her that he had been a strong leader who at times seemed more like a manipulative bully than a good parish priest. But they pointed out that when Canon King was around, you knew where you were. Things got done. People were clear what was expected of them. Janice, one of the churchwardens, summed up how she saw the problem: 'Yes, we said we wanted a pastor and we really do; but we also need a rector who can hold us together, keep us apart sometimes, and lead us forward. We don't want another Canon King, but . . .'

Learning to talk

How should we talk about the people we are called to serve and lead? The languages and cultures of the market economy have influenced the churches as well as other voluntary organizations. Why not just allow designations such as 'client', 'customer' or 'service user' to become our standard ways of referring to the people we serve and lead? After all, these express how many people actually relate to the clergy. Parents seeking baptism, couples planning weddings and people arranging funerals are all service users and in relation to them the church and clergy are service providers. They are seeking an efficient, friendly, professional piece of work and we are expected to provide it. This user–provider dynamic is also present in the expectation-set of people who regularly come to worship and participate in the organizational life of the church. They might be a bit hazy about what their clergy are supposed to be and do when they aren't leading worship or church groups, but they certainly think the clergy themselves ought to be clear about this. They expect the clergy to work to professional standards and they feel that they have a right to complain when they don't.

In the Church of England this is reinforced by a whole raft of legislation from national government and from the Archbishops' Council. Child Protection, Disability Discrimination, Employment Law, Charities Law, Clergy Code of Conduct, Clergy Discipline Measure, Clergy Terms and Conditions of Service, Ministry Development Review and Continuing Ministerial Development requirements have all fuelled expectations that the clergy will routinely operate to professional standards of work, behaviour and accountability. There are good reasons why the Church should warmly welcome these developments. We definitely do not need less professionally aware clergy pastoring and leading the twenty-first-century Church in mission and ministry. However, we must also realize that we are living with a major culture shift in the Church where there seems to be little room left for the old tradition of the 'holy companion' type of pastor, still less for the amiable, bungling, and largely ineffectual 'holy amateur'. At the same time as we are called to be locally and publicly holy and human we are expected to be professional about what we profess. This, with major changes in church economics, all leads to a much more 'managerial' culture in relationships between clergy and people and between clergy and those who call and lead them. This in turn leads to reinterpretations of the basic dynamics of ministry practice so that many clergy are coming to see their work, and even their personal spirituality, as an unending series of project management exercises (though they rarely express it explicitly in these terms). This kind of cultural and institutional development is likely to have a strong influence on the way we think and therefore the way we speak about the people we lead and serve. If this 'project management' dynamic of ministry is allowed simply to continue without being subjected to careful theological reflection, it can suck the spiritual guts out of the clergy as well as of the churches they lead. The 'language' of the gospel and the language of those who lead in ministry can become foreign tongues to each other without anybody really noticing that it is happening.

Henry is the rector of a major town-centre church where everything in ministry is done very well – high-quality music and liturgy, superbly managed parish office, lots of groups for young and old. This is a high-status parish from which in the past some of the incumbents have gone on to be bishops. Henry says that he is proud to be the rector of such an important parish, and his projects are all going well, but he wonders what kind of priest he is becoming. I asked him how long it was since he had actually sat down and really listened to, and offered to pray with, a member of his church. He didn't answer that question, but went on to confess how lonely and spiritually sterile he had been feeling for months. He feels trapped into the pace and values of the organizational life of his church, but finds it less and less easy to see the connection between all this activism and the values of the gospel that he knows in his heart of hearts should be challenging them. Henry is certainly in a leadership role, but what kind of leadership is he actually called by God to exercise in that place?

How we talk about the people we serve and lead is not just a random choice of equally valid expressions. The rhetoric we use describes the kind of relationships that we believe we are involved in. It embodies the values that we really hold. Tim, whom we met in Chapter 5, probably said a lot more than he realized when he described his church people as 'a bunch of thick teenagers'. He liked to go to the pub for a drink with Jacqui, a neighbouring priest. In their conversation he often jokingly referred to the people at his church as 'the kiddy-winkies'. After a time Jacqui asked him, 'Do you think you should really be talking about them like that? Is that how you really think of them?' How we speak in unguarded moments can reveal truths that we are normally careful to keep under wraps, even from ourselves.

There are lots of excellent books describing leadership styles and strategies the clergy might adopt to shape our ministries, so I don't propose to rehearse these here. Most of them draw on business models, but few of them really dwell on the theology of relationships between leader and led.[9] This is important because nearly all models of leadership in business that have been taken up in writing about Christian ministry are based on how power relationships can best be configured and managed to get the aims of the organization delivered most effectively. There is a lot that is right about this, but it does leave me with a question. Can we find a theological model that will help us understand the kind of relationship between the priest as servant and leader and the people of the priest's church? I am looking for a way of talking about this relationship that has enough room in it to embody the core values of the gospel of Christ *and* enough security to learn from 'secular' insights about leadership. It needs to be robust enough to hold firm to the essential identity and purpose of Christian ministry. At the same time it needs to be able to cope with the organizational challenges of local churches where most of the action is carried out by volunteers, not employees. I propose that a biblical 'model' of *friendship* could provide this framework.

Friends

In John 15 Jesus calls his disciples his friends. He is talking to them about who they are and who he is (identity); about fruitfulness (purpose); about the linkage between what he says and what they are to do (authority); about the energy that will take them where he calls them (motivation); and about how far he will have to go (and they may have to go) to achieve the task (cost). It should be clear from this that Jesus' idea of friendship and the wider biblical teaching about friendship describe a spiritually, emotionally and practically robust relationship. Ordinary human friendship can go very deep, be profoundly intimate and be faithfully maintained through good times and bad for a lifetime. But human friendships can also be shallow, based on superficial warmth of acquaintance, and transient under the pressures and circumstances of life.

I have often wondered why in this part of John's Gospel Jesus talks of his disciples as his friends rather than, say, as his brothers and sisters. After all, he encourages his disciples to understand his and their relationship with God in terms of parenthood. Even when he does use family language to describe his disciples (for example, Mark 3.35), he says in effect that the real proof that you are in a family relationship with God is where God's will stacks up with how you live. It is clear that Jesus' choice of friendship language in John 15 is deliberate. I suggest four reasons for this which will help with our thinking about clergy being called to lead as well as to serve. They connect the kind of friendship Jesus is talking about with freedom, loyalty, knowledge and wisdom – all of them basic to a real Christian understanding of the relationship between leaders and the people they lead. I will reflect on each of these briefly, then add a fifth, the presence or absence of which literally makes all the difference in the world to how Christian ministry may be experienced in practice.

Freedom

Freedom is basic to real friendship. As the cliché goes, you are landed with your family, but you choose your friends. Jewish teachers of Jesus' time were very used to having disciples who came to them for a period, stayed to learn what they could, then moved on to another teacher when their needs changed. Mostly the disciples chose their rabbis or teachers. But Jesus turns this around and tells his disciples, 'You did not choose me but I chose you' (John 15.16). He brings together two things that make for freedom in the relationship between leaders and led – calling and choice. Jesus calls and the disciples can choose whether or not to accept his choice of them. This is important when it comes to the evidence of friendship with Jesus – obedience to his commands. Jesus does not teach that friendship with him is conditional on obedience to his teaching. Rather he is saying that obedience to what he teaches will come naturally out of friendship with him. There is a difference between these two understandings that has major implications for the leadership relationship. The difference is between a leader–disciple relationship that is edgy and insecure, where approval is dependent on performance, and one that is so secure, well-founded and liberating that the friendship expresses it through joint commitment to shared aims; where there is room for imagination, questioning and risk-taking. The teacher and disciple can keep travelling the road together, hard as it can become, because they have come together in a friendship that has the quality of freedom for both of them. This freedom of friendship is essential for the fruitfulness of the relationship between teacher and disciple.

Loyalty

Loyalty is the core commitment that characterizes biblical ideas of friendship. Loyalty to the needs and the will of the other person expresses the depth of the friendship between them. Loyalty in friendship can sometimes sit uncomfortably with the claims of family loyalty: 'the soul of Jonathan was bound to the soul of David, and Jonathan loved him as his own soul', we are told in 1 Samuel 18.1. Their friendship led to Jonathan having to choose between obedience to his father King Saul and protecting David from life-threatening harm. Jonathan's loyalty to David grows out of the context of personal affection, even intimacy. Although they were of unequal status – Jonathan the king's son and David the servant/fugitive – their friendship levelled this out, so that as the story is told there emerges a kind of parity between them. A very different dynamic of friendship and loyalty is provided by the way the Lord is described as speaking with Moses in Exodus 33.11: 'Thus the LORD used to speak to Moses face to face, as one speaks to a friend.' Moses has to go into the holy tabernacle to meet with the Lord. There is no question here of parity between the friends who are meeting. The 'roles' are clear, the friendship is close and strong, and loyalty (faithfulness) is at the heart of the relationship.

The connection between faithfulness and the actions that express it are highlighted by James: ' "Abraham believed God, and it was reckoned to him as righteousness", and he was called the friend of God' (2.23). Pontius Pilate finds himself trapped in a similar loyalty–action dynamic, though in a much more coercive, fearful and sinister context, as he is warned, 'If you release this man, you are no friend of the emperor' (John 19.12). It should be clear that there is a big difference between the faith dynamics of Abraham's and Moses' friendship with God and Pilate's 'friendship' with Caesar! However, the point is clear enough. When Jesus speaks about the connection between friendship and obedience to what he says in John 15.14 he is drawing on the Abraham/Moses tradition of friendship with God that expresses itself in loyalty and faithfulness to God's will.

Just as there is no question that Jesus' disciples related to him as their leader, there is also no question that Jesus wanted to change their ideas of what that leadership must mean. Jesus confronts the disciples after James and John have made their power bid: 'You know that the rulers of the Gentiles lord it over them . . . It will not be so among you; but whoever wishes to be great among you must be your servant, and whoever wishes to be first among you must be your slave' (Matthew 20.25–27). John shows Jesus driving this point home after he has washed his disciples' feet: 'You call me Teacher and Lord – and you are right, for that is what I am. So if I, your Lord and Teacher, have washed your feet, you also ought to wash one another's feet' (John 13.13–14).

This most basic lesson for Jesus' disciples has big implications for how clergy and church members see the role of leadership in ministry. That Jesus sets such store by loyalty to his will and his ways when he describes those he has chosen as his friends is compelling witness to the kind of community and the kind of leadership within it he is calling them to. The challenge for clergy and other people in church leadership is – to put it bluntly: do we believe the gospel Jesus teaches or don't we? In biblical terms believing is about what you do with your body, not just about what you do with your mind, however apparently holy that seems to be. For the people Jesus calls friends, loyalty to his will and his ways is likely to lead to some stretching rethinking of what being leaders in the community of God's people involves. And this could also be stretching for the people who are being led.

Bishop Richard stayed on to greet the candidates and their families over a buffet after the confirmation service. When most people had gone he disappeared from the main hall and joined the people in the kitchen doing the washing up. 'It's not right and I don't like it!' one of them complained to me. 'He should be being a proper bishop instead of coming into our kitchen. You'd better tell him!'

Knowledge

Jesus connects the friendship he has with his disciples with the knowledge he shares with them. He contrasts the master–servant relationship with the kind of friendship that he is offering: 'I do not call you servants any longer, because the servant does not know what the master is doing; but I have called you friends, because I have made known to you everything that I have heard from my Father' (John 15.15). There are echoes here of God speaking with Moses as with a friend. This conversation is about far more than sharing information or giving instructions. It is the opening of the mind of God to the disciples through Jesus opening his mind to them. This kind of 'making known' does not just carry the leadership function of information disclosure and task-sharing. It is about trustful person-to-person sharing and appropriate self-disclosure.

Further on in the conversation Jesus shows that what he has shared does not amount to a total disclosure of all that has taken place or of everything that will happen. 'I still have many things to say to you, but you cannot bear them now' (John 16.12). As he gets ready to face the biggest task of all, Jesus is well aware of the limitations of his disciples. At the moment they simply cannot take in everything he wants them to know. This is obviously not because Jesus doesn't trust them to make good use of what he could tell them, but because he loves them so much and knows them so well that he is clear about the amount that they can take on board at this particular time. Jesus' whole orientation towards his disciples is to include them in his knowledge of who the Father is and what the Father is doing. There is more to be said than can usefully be said right now. So Jesus promises provision for their further learning as he tells them, 'When the Spirit of truth comes, he will guide you into all the truth . . . he will take what is mine and declare it to you' (16.13–15). Even then, as becomes clear later on, Jesus seems to have overestimated the capacity of his disciples to live in the present with the kind of knowledge he has been sharing with them. Nevertheless he loves them enough to take the risk and trust them with what he has to say.

The Bible starts with God speaking. It is filled with stories of God speaking to and through key people at key times. Hebrews starts by recalling that 'Long ago God spoke to our ancestors in many and various ways by the prophets, but in these last days he has spoken to us by a Son, whom he appointed heir of all things . . .' The most developed theological statement in the Bible about Jesus calls him God's 'Word'. As generations of bloggers, Facebookers and tweeters have discovered, sometimes to their cost, those who speak must take the risk of how they will be heard and what will be done with what they say. God takes the risks of speech. Jesus is what God has to say.

In the Bible the speaking of God is mostly about knowledge and invitation. God wants people to know who he is, what he is for, what he is doing; and he wants them to join in – that is what 'covenant theology' is all about. In the Bible God just will not shut up. God is love and so he must speak. This does not arise from some inadequacy in God's character that makes him speak inappropriately in the way that often happens with leaders of churches and other organizations. It simply arises from the fact that God loves, so God speaks and trusts people with what he has to say. These are some of the characteristics of the kind of friendship Jesus wants to have with his disciples – where he loves them enough to trust them with what the Father has been giving to him. The fact that God speaks does not stop him being God – it simply shows what kind of God he is – any more than Jesus sharing his knowledge of the Father with his friends stands in the way of their being his disciples and he their Lord.

I am well aware that what I have been writing here will ring alarm bells with people who are uneasy about the kind of role confusion that can arise between clergy and church members through inappropriate sharing of information and indiscriminate self-disclosure. Inappropriate information-giving or unwise self-disclosure can indeed be destructive in the relationship between clergy as church leaders and their fellow Christians. Fear of this possibility is what lies behind the warnings given in seminaries (even today!) about the dangers of having close friends among members of your own congregation. It should be clear enough that anybody in leadership will have to take account of the person–role dynamic that will best express the values, purposes and actions of their organization. I will highlight this later. Nevertheless, the oft-repeated prohibition on the clergy having friendships in the churches they serve can be demoralizing for the clergy and for the people we serve – it can seem as if there is to be one gospel that we preach for the people and a different (or more restricted) one for the clergy.

In every church and community where I have served as a priest I have found people who have become good friends – people I love and people who I know love me. Sometimes we share leisure time together – watching cricket, playing golf (a great leveller!), eating together. Good-quality, non-intrusive friendships like these are treasure. As I finally get out of a golf bunker at the sixth attempt my partner says, 'You seem to have a lot on your mind right now. It's affecting your game.' I respond with a grunt, 'Yes, that's how it is at the moment', and we continue walking together. It is enough. I have a good network of other friends too – people I can really trust and who also really pray.

A major leadership role involves the management of information and knowledge – becoming clear about its validity or its relevance and having the skills and awareness of how best to communicate it, to whom and when. There is a lot of difference between the 'mushroom farming' approach to leadership – keep them in the dark and throw muck all over them – and helping people to have knowledge that they can use and light to see where it is all heading for. Clergy who are insecure (we all are to some extent!) can withhold or fail to communicate important knowledge in order to boost their own self-importance or increase people's dependency on them as church leaders. The distortions that can result from this are obvious – among them the assumption that the clergy are the leaders who have all or most of the knowledge needed to move a church forwards; if only they would share it. This leads to my fourth characteristic of the kind of friendship Jesus is expressing as he teaches his disciples – wisdom.

Wisdom

In the Bible the role of Wisdom is to show the connections between the purposes of God and the practical realities of day-to-day life. Wisdom is portrayed as a woman calling out in the streets for people to listen to what she has to say, because if they do it will change how they see things and the way they live. John's Gospel has lots of echoes with the wisdom literature of the Bible – especially the way John portrays Jesus as the revealer of the truth that people are called to follow. Wisdom has a special passion for making people beloved (*philoi*, friends) of God. The Jesuit New Testament scholar Raymond Brown puts it like this: 'In making men his *philoi* through his union with them Jesus is acting in the manner of divine Wisdom: "In every generation she passes into holy souls and makes them the beloved (*philoi*) of God"' (Wisdom 7.27).[10] Holy Wisdom draws near to speak God's message about who people really are, what they are called to be towards one another, what they are called to do. The fact that in some of the biblical wisdom books God is comparatively rarely mentioned specifically has led people down the centuries to see in Wisdom herself a portrayal of God calling out to those she would have as her friends.

From this briefest of sketches it should be clear that the wisdom I am describing as a characteristic of the friendship Jesus is calling for is far deeper than the accumulation of years of experience and practical know-how. There can be real wisdom in leaders who have been able to learn from experience and hone their people skills and practice in the 'school of hard knocks'. But the wisdom that energizes the friends of God goes further and deeper. It does connect with practical action and getting on with the job in hand. As a characteristic of the friends of God it stimulates ways of looking that can really catch sight of what God is wanting to do, and ways of living that have the capacity to bring people and God together in the same place and at the same time – at first perhaps for a moment or two, but little by little as a matter of habit. Holy Wisdom does this because she is a person, not just a set of principles. Friendship with Jesus comes alive for the disciples when Wisdom gets up close and personal with them with the arrival of the Holy Spirit that Jesus promises.

These four characteristics of friendship with Jesus that I have been talking about – freedom, loyalty, knowledge, wisdom – are all deeply attractive. Reflection on them can warm our jaded souls and attract us to seek refreshment and renewal in our discipleship and ministry. They are also easily corruptible by human selfishness and fallibility. These don't take long to come to the surface when the pressures of ministry become really intense and the time we have available to spend really attending to people is a lot shorter than the long list of needs we are supposed to meet.

Love

Our ministries can be exhilarating and exhausting and lots in-between. Most clergy will know the experience of preaching the grace, peace and generosity of God in Christ while inwardly feeling absolutely frazzled. This can happen because of the peaks and troughs of ministry, and also because of what we are dealing with at particular times. To date, one of the worst weeks in my own ministry was when I found myself dealing with funerals following a cot death, a murder and a suicide all in one week at the same time as my church council was having a row about whether to hire a marquee for the forthcoming garden party. But it doesn't have to be as dramatic as that – and, thank God, it normally isn't. As I write this a Zimbabwean priest has just been visiting our church. He told me that a joke among his colleagues is that the Church of England is all about 'matters arising'. 'At every meeting of your churches we go to people spend more time talking about matters arising than about anything else – that's why you never seem to get anything done!' He has a point. Often local church ministry can be utterly tedious in ways that would sap the spiritual energy of a grade one saint, let alone the local Reverend Bloggins. A clergy friend of mine has a sticker next to his desk: 'I love God – it's Christians I can't stand!' Occasionally I have wanted to go further than that. I think it is true that since I first turned to Christ as a teenager I have never quite stopped believing in God, but there have been times when I have wished that he would just ****** off for a while and leave me alone. When ministry hurts that much, it matters that you know who you are serving, what he thinks of you, and that you just offer what you can – in Christ it will be enough. It also matters that you have well-rooted confidence in the grace that is perfected in weakness (2 Corinthians 12.9).

Damian had already been vicar of two small parishes before he was appointed as minister of a large church in a wealthy residential area. He was proud of his new appointment and worried about the responsibility of leading this thriving church. He resolved to get up early every morning to pray for everybody on his church membership list every day and always in the same order. After this he was available in the church office, though he was surprised that not many people came to see him. The church ticked along and Damian kept on with his prayer routine for month after month. Soon he began to feel very anxious, so much so that if he lost his place in the list of people he was praying for (there were several hundred of them on it) he would start again from the beginning until he had got everybody prayed for in exactly the right order.

On the surface his ministry appeared to be going well, but within himself Damian grew more and more lonely and more desperate as he ploughed through this obsessive compulsive daily prayer routine. Eventually he came for help. He told me that he was very conscious of working for God and wanted to aim for the highest standards. He prayed devotedly, worked hard, ensured that his teaching and preaching were well researched, prayed through and well delivered. Several times in this first conversation he said that he was determined to give his ministry everything he'd got. I found him a very impressive priest and church leader. But . . .

When I asked him what he thought of God, he gave me the conventional answer that he loved the Lord and had always wanted nothing more than to serve him as well as possible. I stopped him and asked him again what he really thought of God. After a long silence he told me almost in a whisper that he hated God. He'd tried all his life to please God, but nothing he did ever seemed enough. The only way he knew how to keep God off his back (his words) was to keep on working harder and harder to higher and higher standards. I asked him what he thought of his parishioners. Again, after the conventional answers, he admitted that he was afraid of many of them – he had a dreadful inner fear of being 'found out' so he put on the best front that he could and was pleased that so many of them seemed to value his ministry. Within himself he felt excruciatingly lonely at the same time as allowing nobody among his parishioners, or even within his own family, to get really close to him.

To outsiders Damian was a successful church leader, appreciated by his people, godly in his conduct, a prayerful and conscientious minister of the gospel. He appeared to be a 'friend of God' – loyal, knowledgeable, wise. In fact he was courting serious trouble emotionally, mentally, spiritually and in other ways. Like many Christian ministers Damian had lost sight of the most basic reality of Christian discipleship and ministry, and therefore of the most basic value of authentic church leadership – that all of it starts from the love of God, is sustained by the love of God and is there to open the doors to the love of God in a world that is desperately short of that kind of love.

Jesus' teaching about faithfulness and fruitfulness, as we have it in John 15, is all about love. What makes this love effective in reality rather than some kind of pious fantasy is *connection*. As church leaders we can no more minister the authentic grace of God to people apart from our connection to Jesus than a vine branch that has been severed from the main plant can produce a bunch of grapes. The one thing that distinguishes the people and leaders of God's Church from leaders of other organizations is the absolute requirement for radical connectedness to Jesus Christ. The power that makes that connection, keeps it alive and renews it is the power of love. When we understand church leadership primarily in terms of organizational development and project management, however much we dress this up in language about spirituality and mission, we risk parting company with the most basic principles of Christian discipleship and ministry. We risk becoming manipulators and exploiters of people, rather than ministers who love the people enough to call them to join in the company of those Jesus calls his friends.

It can be helpful to think of most of the New Testament letters as being addressed directly to church leaders (I am aware of the anachronism that this phraseology implies!). I imagine that they were sent to the leaders of churches to be read to the members and learned from by leaders and people together. They can be thought of as foundation texts for church leadership. Probably the simplest example is 1 Corinthians. The three chapters 12 to 14, about holding together the unity of the church as 'the body of Christ', focus directly on attitudes and actions that are central to the calling of church leaders. The central part of this section is the great 'hymn of love' in 1 Corinthians 13. I think that it is fair to interpret this in its context as a key text about church leadership as well as being about Christian discipleship. Without the kind of love characterized by Paul in chapter 13, the unity and effectiveness of the body of Christ looked for in the previous chapter can be no more than an unfulfilled faith claim or a permanently deferred hope. The generosity that makes space for all members to offer their distinctive contributions and have them recognized as gifts from the heart of God could be no more than a wistful fantasy. The purpose of the gospel is to open the way to the Father through Jesus in the grace of the Holy Spirit. Only the love that lasts will make this possible. For me the promise of verse 12 goes to the heart of it – 'For now we see in a mirror, dimly, but then we will see face to face. Now I know only in part; then I will know fully, even as I have been fully known.' With this love there is no place to hide because there is no need to hide.

Contrast this quality of the love of God in Jesus with the tyrannical, demanding, ever dissatisfied, always-on-your-back figure that Damian (and some other clergy in my experience) has struggled to satisfy through his punishing work and prayer schedules. This merciless 'God' is far more clearly a projection of the cleric's own inner fears, anxieties and insecurities than anything remotely to do with God in Jesus Christ. This false god has been given spiritual and emotional house room for so long that it has grown slowly into a resident idol masquerading as God. It would surely be far better for Damian and others like him to become atheists rather than keep on trying to believe in, preach about and serve that kind of 'god'. To borrow a very helpful expression of Philip Yancey, what is needed by Damian and, I believe, by many of us who are called to lead, is to 'meet Jesus again for the first time', and to go with him again and again into the welcoming presence of God who loves without limit. It is within this love that Jesus calls his disciples not servants, but friends.

I am aware that what I have written in most of this chapter so far could be thought of as ignoring the shapes of leadership dynamics and avoiding tough issues by over-spiritualizing them. I don't think I have done this, but still the question must be faced. How is all this supposed to relate to the lessons to be learned from organizational leadership theories and methods? There are many excellent books and organizations dedicated to exploring best practice in church leadership – I particularly recommend the work of the Foundation for Church Leadership.[11] For the moment, with what I have offered in this chapter so far as foundation, I will explore just one issue that is basic to leadership in any church. This concerns how the relationship between person, role and boundary might bear on our ability to cope with sudden or persistent pressure when we are leading our communities through times of change.

In Figure 1, the person and the role overlap almost completely. When the pressure comes on the role, the priest is likely to 'take it personally'. The minister is likely to have an overly strong personal investment in the change being sought and to see those who engage in passive or active resistance to the change as opposing his or her leadership (or even resisting God's plans) by being disloyal, awkward or worse. There is insufficient critical distance for the minister to be able to hear properly what it is about the proposed change that is being resisted and why. Paranoid leadership dynamics can foster a culture of confrontation that makes change and development easy to start and hard to sustain. Friendships valued by this leader are likely to be close, deep and exclusive, giving rise to well-founded worries about the 'vicar's clique'.

Christopher made it clear that he wanted to move his rather traditional church of St Peter's into charismatic renewal. Four

Figure 1 Person and role almost the same – 'My ministry is my life'

young couples who had recently transferred to St Peter's after a split in St John's over charismatic renewal encouraged him in this. He saw them as his real allies in taking his church forward at last. He became angry, depressed and disoriented when his proposal that the whole PCC should attend a New Wine renewal weekend met with solid resistance, and soon afterwards the four new couples moved on to another church.

In Figure 2 there is such a distance between the person and the role that when the pressure comes the minister hardly appears to notice. The person of the minister is inaccessible to the people. This can lead to the people feeling overridden – 'the clergy will get their way whatever we say' – or feeling ignored – 'they don't care so we won't care'. The distance between person and role is too great to be critically creative. Either way, active and passive resistance to change is not allowed its voice, key questions have no way of being properly heard, and people feel manipulated or devalued. The foundations for a culture of divisiveness and competitiveness in the local church are firmly laid. Friendship is excluded from the minister–people relationship.

James liked to keep his personal preferences and his ministerial life completely separate. Although he smiled regularly when on duty

Figure 2 Person and role too far apart – 'Ministry is just a job like any other job'

and appeared friendly, people found him unapproachable, not only about their pastoral needs but even about practical things. He used email a lot in relation to administrative matters, even with church people he came into contact with very frequently. When his churchwardens asked why he didn't join in more with his church's social events he told them, 'My door is always open for people who want to see me.' However, few of them wanted to bother.

In Figure 3, person and role are close enough to spark with each other, but also sufficiently distinctive to be able to cope with difference. There is enough space – 'critical distance' – for active and passive resistances to be properly heard and interpreted. Proposals can be changed in the light of new data that can be properly evaluated. The minister is accessible to the people – they can get to know and trust one another enough to move forward together, sharing the risks of change with hearts, eyes and hands open. There is room for friendship to grow which recognizes and respects the variety of roles and relationships.

This is a useful model to highlight an important issue, but it is too crude to do much more than that. Relationships between clergy and their churches are not just binary – one priest relating to one lay person about one thing at a time – they take place within

Figure 3 Person and role in right balance – 'We are together in this ministry'

overlapping systems or networks of relationships, power bids, groups with different motives and needs. Nevertheless, getting our person and role into right balance (something that has to be done repeatedly) is basic to being able to respond well to the opportunities and challenges of being called to lead.

It should be clear that for ministers to be free to hold person and role in right balance they need to be sufficiently secure not only about who they really are, *but about the worthwhileness of who they really are*. Damian, the minister who admitted to his hatred of 'God', in fact had a very low level of self-esteem. His admitted hatred of 'God' was closely related to his self-hatred, which he projected outwards, then denied so that it was almost always suppressed. It just lay there, eating away at his self-worth. His energetic engagement with his ministry was partly designed to help him keep up the denial of a truth about himself that he found dreadfully hard to face.

Jesus' designation of his disciples as friends (not servants or slaves) characterizes them as utterly beloved. This is the foundational truth of who they really are before God. Who we are before God is who we really are. This kind of love sets Jesus' friends free to become who they are called to be, to go where he sends them and to embrace with both faith and realism the risks involved in becoming leaders of the people of God in the mission of God.

The freedom of knowing ourselves to be truly loved and called to friendship with God in Christ is liberating for those who struggle with understanding their role in relation to one piece of ministry activity or another. This is not because personal worth functions as a kind of consolation prize when things are difficult with the role – 'My church people hate me but that's all right because God loves me!' Not at all. The freedom of knowing oneself to be in friendship with God in Christ releases spiritual and emotional energy and discernment that can enable proper engagement with role and boundary issues that has no need for instinctive defensiveness, double-speak or evasiveness.

I am *not* saying that all clergy who struggle with their ministries suffer from intractably poor self-image and distorted spiritualities, though it is clear that many of us do. Some ministries would be very difficult even if the Angel Gabriel were the vicar and St Francis the curate! Nor am I saying that getting our understanding of the spirituality of ministerial leadership as based in friendship with Jesus right will guarantee a happy and successful ministry. But I do think that Jesus' designation of his disciples – the soon-to-be leaders of his people – as friends has the potential to open up new understandings of key agendas of church leadership involving identity, purpose, authority, motivation, direction, resources and cost. I do not believe that there is a simple key that opens the door to getting this right and then all problems will be solved. There are lessons here to be learned and relearned until we get to heaven. One of the most important of these concerns God's call to rest and to wait.

To reflect on and talk about

1 How do you think about and talk about the people you minister to and share ministry with?
2 How for you could friendship relate to leadership in local churches that you know?
3 Of the three diagrams about person and role, which is closest to how you experience fellow ministers and the way they relate themselves to their work?
4 What questions does Damian's story raise for you about leadership and friendship with God and with people?

7

Called to rest and wait

Without the capacity to rest and wait, the call to belong can degenerate into craving for affirmation and approval; the call to be holy can degenerate into religiosity and eccentricity; the call to be human can degenerate into inappropriate self-protectiveness; the call to serve can lead to anxiety-driven activism; and the call to lead can construct mission and ministry as project management with criteria for success and failure that miss the heart of the gospel by a mile.

Some parts of the Christian message are easier to teach and preach than they are to model and practise – forgiveness, gentleness, living by grace, loving neighbours and enemies are just a few examples. The call to rest and wait is like that too. In churches where people have insatiable desires to be recognized, respected, loved, cared for and affirmed, the demands on leaders to be frantically activist in 'delivering the goods' is enormous and often impossibly hard to resist. As the following two stories show, the pressures can be self-induced or they can come at us in the form of expectations thrown up by our ministry settings. Most often they are a combination of both.

When Victor started his ministry as a new bishop he was a man in a tremendous hurry. He arrived in a diocese where the churches and clergy felt starved of affirming pastoral care. Victor stated his intention of visiting every priest in the diocese in their own homes for at least half an hour within his first four months. Following that, he would carry through a programme of visits to community groups and organizations and hold high-profile public seminars where people could come and fire any question they liked about faith and public life and he would respond. He achieved this programme and carried on with a pace of inspirational ministry that left his staff tired out with trying to keep up with him. When he wasn't engaged in visiting churches and community groups he made himself available for personal consultation by the clergy and people of the diocese. Many who went to him spoke of his kindness, careful listening, patience, prayerfulness and practical helpfulness.

Nine months after Victor started as bishop he began to miss appointments or delegate them at very short notice to members of his staff. His office said that Bishop Victor had injured his back while gardening. Gradually he missed more appointments and the diocese was asked to pray for him as he received further treatment for his very painful and debilitating back problem. On one of his church visits he appeared to be preoccupied, he repeatedly asked what he was expected to do, his hands trembled and he seemed to be on the verge of tears. He was clearly moving into a major personal crisis of some kind. During the several months that this went on, his office put out regular statements saying the Bishop's back trouble had got worse, he was taking time off work, and asking people to pray.

Wills, who was a priest in the diocese and was also on the verge of a breakdown, confided to a friend, 'I know that back trouble can really wear you down and I honestly do feel sorry for him, but the message is clear enough, isn't it? If you can't cope you'd better have back trouble, but you mustn't let the side down by having a breakdown – so what the hell am *I* supposed to do with all *my* misery?'

Eventually Victor was able to return to his ministry as a bishop. The spiritual spark that people found so attractive was still there, but he was less exhausting to be with. He did a lot less rushing around, but seemed more available to people. He spoke honestly about what had happened to him. The clergy and people of the diocese came to respect him, even to love him, and to find in him the kind of pastor and leader in mission they had needed for so long. For those who felt vulnerable and under pressure, the diocese began to feel a safer place to be.

Victor's story is about a driven person who became a victim of the unrealistically heavy demands he made on himself. But the pace and demands of local church ministry can wear down even people who take a wiser and more balanced approach to their ministries than Victor was able to.

Emma was a senior training consultant before ordination and delivered a lot of clergy training around themes such as work–life balance, team dynamics, and mentoring relationships. She thrived in ministry during her three years as curate of a lively church in a dockland regeneration area. After three months as vicar of a group of four churches, each with its own patterns of services and meetings, she felt worn out by the experience of being on a treadmill of work that demanded that she just kept on going, kept on delivering, and that gave her no time to really pray, think or plan. She asked herself what all this activity was supposed to be achieving for the gospel, whether the pace would ever let up, and whether there would ever be time for her to engage in the careful and prayerful reflection about ministry that she so effectively commended to others.

Reading these two stories, many more clergy will hear echoes of their experience in Emma's situation than in Victor's, but both stories are surprisingly common. For everyone like Victor who actually succumbed to a breakdown, there are many more who somehow barely manage to just hold back from going 'over the edge'. This is an unhealthy and disturbing feature of ordained ministry in which over-demanding lay people and senior church leaders too often collude with the natural over-activism of many of the clergy themselves. This is not the place to go into the vastly unrealistic work demands created by changing configurations of parishes without engaging properly with the theological and pastoral task of reshaping the mission and pastoral care of the clergy. However, we do need to be clear that churches that develop unhealthy patterns of ministry are often at serious risk of undermining the credibility of the gospel that we are here to demonstrate and commend.

A lot of energetic and genuinely fruitful ministerial activity comes from people who live from high levels of nervous energy. When they are in prominent positions of leadership they can influence the whole culture of their church or team for good or ill (usually both). They can become role models whose core message seems to be, 'If you are going to be a real Christian round here you need to keep up and do it like I do.' However, as Jesus' selection of his first disciples shows us, God does not demand that we belong to a particular personality type or social group for him to use us effectively in ministry. Indeed, some of the most effective ministry is offered by people who have significant areas of vulnerability in their character make-up, their experience or their circumstances. They are unable to rush about to do God's work, or they have learned not to. People who do a lot of pastoral work with clergy see a great deal of evidence that apparently fruitful (and often genuinely fruitful) ministries can have behind them deep levels of personal anxiety and, as we saw in Damian, deep-rooted anger towards God for calling them in the first place. It is all too easy even for the best of us to lose sight of the principle, emphasized in Chapter 6, that genuine Christian ministry starts with love, is sustained by love and has the call of love as its main task and purpose. This means that a major call for the clergy is to become people who know what it is to practise resting and waiting. If we are actually going to live our ministries like that we need to have a rather special understanding of God's gifts of time and place.

Time

The creation stories in Genesis 1—2 have a sense of purpose, rhythm, fruitfulness, pattern and pace. God speaks, the word bears fruit, patterns emerge where everything fits together, each part of the creation has identity and is 'in place'. The nurturing rhythm of time itself as part of creation is emphasized by the poetic repetition: 'And there was evening and there was morning...' The speaking of God, the fruitfulness of what is created by God's word, the rhythms of time and the progression of what God brings into being are all framed within the gift of time. The rhythms and patterns of this first creation story lead to a surprising climax – not, 'Now we've got everything ready let's roll up our sleeves and get on with some work'(!) but, 'And on the seventh day God finished the work that he had done, and he rested... So God blessed the seventh day and hallowed it, because on it God rested from all the work that he had done in creation' (Genesis 2.2–3).

As we saw earlier, many Old Testament scholars link the editing of these Genesis creation stories with the period of Israel's exile in Babylon. The purpose of this was to bring good news and hope to the exiles through drawing on these themes in the preaching and teaching of their community leaders and prophets. Exiles are people who are out of place and out of time – at the mercy of other people's priorities of how time and energy should be spent and used. The experience of exile can include living on the edge of disorder and chaos, never being able to feel quite at home with where you are or who you are. Time and place can be out of joint. This idea and experience of exile can have strong echoes with people who feel under pressure because of the demands of other people or of their own drivenness. Victor, Emma and many others find themselves living by a timetable and running at a pace that they can neither control nor keep up with. They find themselves oppressed by the uncomfortable and lonely exile of contexts and timings imposed by other people or by themselves.

Two Old Testament scholars, von Rad and Brueggemann, capture in their different ways the sense in which God's resting on the seventh day of creation comes as good news to people who are exiled by distorted senses of time and demand. Von Rad says that the text speaks 'of a rest that existed before man and still exists without man's perceiving it. The declaration mounts, as it were, to the place of God himself and testifies that with the living God there is rest.'[12] Brueggemann says:

> ... the observance of the Sabbath had special significance for exiled Israelites. It was an act which announced their faith in this God and a rejection of all other gods, religions and world views. *The celebration of a day of rest was, then, the announcement of trust in this God who is confident enough to rest.* It was then, and is now an assertion that life does not depend upon our feverish activity of self-securing, but that there can be a pause in which life is given to us simply as a gift.[13]

The sabbath becomes one of the most distinctive hallmarks of the people of God in Scripture. It is included in the commandments given them by God and provided for in their holiness codes to be received and practised wherever they lived. One of the distinctive things about these people of this God is that whatever everybody else did, they were people who rested. This testified to God's intention that time is to be both understood and experienced as gift, not curse.

How the sabbath should be kept was one of the battlegrounds between Jesus and the Pharisees. It seems that over-legalistic application of sabbath regulations was in danger of taking God's gift of time and institutionalizing it by making a separation between sabbath time and 'ordinary' time. The stories about Jesus healing on the sabbath (such as Mark 3.1–6) show him *reconnecting* sabbath time with 'ordinary' time. Mark 3 tells us that from the moment that Jesus and the man with the withered hand came into the synagogue the Pharisees were watching Jesus like a hawk so that they might be able to accuse him. Their response to the healing was not to praise God but to plot how they might kill Jesus. This passage shows that in spite of their devotion and commitment in their service of God some, at least, of the Pharisees were profoundly 'out of time' with God and out of time and place with God's values being demonstrated by Jesus.

Jesus' teaching that 'the sabbath was made for humankind, and not humankind for the sabbath' (Mark 2.27), far from saying that the sabbath can be disregarded, emphasizes its importance. The time-gift of the sabbath points to the true nature of all time in the economy of God – as loving, purposeful gift to be received, valued, treasured, used. We see this in the way that Jesus is shown using time and living 'in time' with God. We see him taking time to discern how to approach his mission, to be with people who need him, sometimes slowing down when he is on the way somewhere else, sometimes striding ahead; we see him making a deliberate delay before going to his friend Lazarus who has died; taking time to sleep in the boat during a storm; taking time out to be quiet and pray; calling his disciples to take time apart so they can rest. As John's Gospel shows, this is far more than Jesus being good at work–life balance or having a fine sense of timing when he is speaking or working with people. In John, Jesus speaks of his 'hour' not yet having come (2.4), the hour that will come (4.23), the hour being ready to come (12.23), the hour having now come (13.1; 17.1). Jesus clearly lived with a deep sense of time, not the time of rushing about, but time that is in close tune with the calling and the purpose of his Father. It seems that the Father's sense of time and Jesus' sense of time (*chairos* – the right time, the appointed time) are in rhythm and harmony with each other. This is all rather different from the situation where we look anxiously at our watches as we rush from place to place, always knowing the time (*chronos*), but rarely 'having' it.

Jesus' sense of time seems closely linked to his sense of identity, belonging and trust. As he addresses God as 'Father' it is clear that he knows who he is himself. He belongs (is in place) in intimate relationship with his Father and he trusts all that he is and does to the Father. Jesus' 'great high priestly prayer' of John 17 starts with Jesus making this affirmation of relationship, timing and trust: 'Father, the hour has come; glorify your Son so that the Son may glorify you.' With the burden Jesus is carrying towards the cross he knows that he is in time with his Father and he can surrender in trust to the Father's will. As the Gethsemane story that follows shows, this does not exempt Jesus from facing up to the suffering and stress that lies ahead – but he faces it with this foundation of a deep, trustful sense of being in time and in place with his Father.

This is not an easy example to follow! One of the great 'promises' of the Old Testament calls out, 'In returning and rest you shall be saved; in quietness and in trust shall be your strength' (Isaiah 30.15). But the context shows this call being made in a situation of turmoil, of political struggle and people battling *against* the call of the Lord! We are not Jesus, but we are called to live our ministries as people who are 'in Christ'. We are called to live and work in this trustful relationship that can give us the sense of quiet confidence that we are in time and in place with God in Christ. And we have to do this in busy churches whose priorities and senses of urgency often show little or no difference from the rest of the frenetic world we live in. This potentially creative tension about time and place is simply part and parcel of the experience of being in public ministry and church leadership. An important question, then, concerns what makes for this tension being creative rather than destructively sapping of morale and energy. Is it possible that even here foolishness can rescue us from the journey towards madness?

We need to be clear. The call to cross the line from activist stress-based ministries and have the confidence to rest and wait, being in time and place with God, is about far more than just happening to be 'in the right place at the right time'. As I will show in Chapter 8, there is an important sense that for our ministries to be authentically *Christian* there will be times when we must be out of joint with our own churches and communities. It is true that our ministries will sometimes be costly. But it is also true that sometimes clergy find ourselves paying the wrong kind of costs at too high a price. It is important, therefore, to be committed to actively practising being 'in time and place with God' in ways that can make ministry more centred, focused and fruitful, and a lot less grim than it sometimes unfortunately is. I will briefly comment in turn on right practice in responsibility, relationship, rest and recreation, and fellowship.

Responsibility

St Matthew's has been well known to successive bishops and their staffs as a graveyard for ministries. In 30 years this isolated parish of light industry, smallholding farms and mobile home parks has seen 11 priests come and go, many of them ministerial misfits before they arrived. The longest stay has been 6 years. Recently the bishop asked Helena to take up the ministry there. She is an experienced priest with a track record of quietly effective service in inner-city parishes. All 11 of her immediate predecessors were appointed to St Matthew's as their first incumbencies. When Helena accepted the bishop's call she told him that while she had always ministered happily in down-market inner urban communities, she had no experience of living and working outside of large towns or with farming communities. She accepted on the two understandings that the bishop would ensure that both she and St Matthew's would be properly supported with prayer, practical resources and training; and that the bishop's staff would engage in serious reflection and active planning about the right shapes of ministry deployment for the whole area of which St Matthew's is a part. To his credit the bishop recognized the wisdom of Helena's 'conditions' for acceptance and is delivering well on his side of the deal. Bishops and others in charge of clergy appointments have a theological and moral obligation to enable clergy to have real opportunity to be in time and place with God by ensuring that the people they call to minister, especially those in very tough circumstances, are properly resourced, sustained and supported. The 'sabbath principle' – the possibility of connecting time, place and practice – needs to be built into the structures of ministry provision and deployment.

Clergy also need to be clear about where our responsibilities lie, and this clarity may not be easy to achieve. 'This is a bad time for you to come to us as rector,' a churchwarden told me on the day I arrived. 'We've just heard that we have to spend £50,000 on the roof.' 'Why is that bad news for me?' I responded. 'You are the churchwarden. I am the parish priest.' We both smiled as we set about learning how best to work together. I am not suggesting that clergy should be 'jobsworths' in relation to particular roles and responsibilities in their parishes. It is not our role to dump on church members and leave them unsupported. But if we are to be in time and in place with God we need to engage with questions of how church leadership, management and governance can relate together so that each enables the others to be as effective as possible. I am not assuming that particular answers to these questions apply in all cases. But if the minister's call to leadership in a particular church includes a substantial expectation of taking the main management role, everybody needs to be honest about this and not just leave it assumed. For myself, I do not believe that the primary role of the clergy should be overly tied up with the detailed management of buildings and organizations. The reality is that for many of us, for much of the time, there is little choice.

Relationship

The responsibility to wait and watch and pray can take different shapes depending on who you are and where you are.

When I became vicar of All Saints, the people in the small congregation came with a long list of things that they wanted me to do – starting a youth group was the first item. I thanked them and promised to worship and work with them to find out how God was calling us to be church together and what he wanted us to do. For the next two years I spent a good part of every working day walking the streets of the parish praying for the people, greeting those I met, spending time in schools, pubs, shops, businesses and factories, down the coal mine, visiting anybody I found at home, trying gently and persistently to construct positive relationships. (For various reasons the church had a difficult history in that community.) In this I was building on some years of the quietly effective pastoral and mission work of my immediate predecessor, Frank, whose ministry had rescued the church from oblivion. Walking the streets didn't feel to me like much of a strategy for church growth. In the meantime I seemed to be burying my congregation faster than new people were coming in. I knew that I must just carry on so I tried to keep on walking, keep on praying, keep on noticing.

As opportunities came through funerals (lots), baptisms (a few), and weddings (rare), I made it a priority to be with the families and neighbours and to pray for them and with them. Quite a lot of the time I felt more bored and frustrated than holy (I have very rarely felt 'holy'). I worried that the bishop would think that I was failing in my ministry because there was so little to show for it. However, Bishop Richard was kind and wise enough to meet me in the parish every few months to pray with me and encourage me to keep on keeping on. Eventually, one by one, then a few at a time, new people began to show up at services, and stay around afterwards to chat over a drink, and little by little the church began to grow again. My ministry at All Saints took a very traditional pastoral mission shape during this long period of waiting and praying – quite different from the church growth strategies I read about in books from successful churches. I wished that I could be like the clergy in those books, but I wasn't and All Saints wasn't like their churches either. I know that many of my colleagues have had to 'walk and wait and pray' for a lot longer than I did there before they see the first signs of new growth.

Don is a natural activist and thrilled to be ordained as a pioneer minister. The challenge of pioneering is that you have to spend most of your time at the frontier, at the margins where roles and responsibilities are less easily described and understood, and often less well regarded than they are at the centre. At first Don found his role of wandering around the town centre, 'being available', very difficult to stay with. But after a while he found three places of quietness that proved to be deeply sustaining for his ministry and surprisingly fruitful for his mission. The first was in the rhythm and routine of the daily services of prayer, meditation and Eucharist in his base church. Although traditional in style (in contrast to Don's charismatic background), they were, he found, places where he had time and space to be with the Lord in the community of prayer. The second was in the corner window of a large pub, where he would sit every day with a coffee and be available to chat with the steady stream of regulars who came in for a warm and a drink. Amid the hubbub of conversation and pub music, Don found a sense of quietness in this place where he was not trying to make anything happen – just be there and available because that's where God called him to be. After a while people expected to find him there and sought him out as their 'vicar'. Relationships were built up where there could be enough trust for conversation that could lead somewhere.

The third place of quietness he found was within himself, and this surprised him. He had been anxious about whether his charismatic church background would make it very difficult for him to adapt to his new church's sacramental style of worship. However, as he found friendship among his colleagues and learned from them about the practice of waiting on God in contemplative prayer, he was aware of becoming quieter within himself and more centred in Christ without, as he put it, 'having to make Jesus happen all the time'. Don had lost none of his energetic spark, but he found himself somehow more free to minister. He began to discover the crucial relationship between prayer as waiting and the practical actions of Christian witness and ministry. He found himself less driven, less anxious. Just as active, but less activist.

All clergy have good reason to know that authentic Christian ministry is about living in the kind of relationship with God in Christ that connects with people because we have time and place for them. Yet the demands of local ministry at a time when the Church is striving to reshape its deployment of clergy as 'focal ministers' and 'missional leaders' can be unremitting. The organizational-induced or self-induced (usually both) pressure to perform easily produces the default position of focusing on organizational rather than relational ministries. Structure and management as key parts of leadership in ministry clearly have their place. Some clergy are called to specialize in organizational and institutional ministries. Through them they are able to influence and resource large sections of the Church in mission, evangelism and pastoral care. Other clergy in strategically important ministries such as chaplains in schools, prisons, hospitals and the military are called to minister in settings where very high levels of organizational awareness and compliance are essential. Whatever the context of our calling, having a deep sense of being in time and in place with God is vital both to our well-being and to the effectiveness of our ministries.

Rest and recreation

The 'sabbath principle' leads to the recommended 'best practice' of the clergy being committed to taking one day per week, preceded where possible by the previous evening, as time off. Until late in the twentieth century the one rest day a week for the general population was enshrined in British law and still deeply embedded in our culture. At least in principle, time had a sense of rhythm. Relaxation of Sunday trading laws, more demanding employment practices and other factors have led to today's 24/7 culture where the weekends are as busy as weekdays, but differently focused on 'leisure' for most people. 'Leisure' time has to contain cleaning, shopping, parenting, fitness, sports, socializing and rest – as well as worship and voluntary service. This piles on the pressure and makes the sabbath principle much more counter-intuitive. For many it seems a really good idea, but over-idealistic and impractical. The sabbath principle can seem very out of joint with 'ordinary time'.

Stipendiary clergy can, officially, count on having at least a day off work every week. The same is not true, at least not in the same way, for many committed lay people who are active in their churches.

For them, their church activities take place in their leisure and volunteer time. This also applies to most self-supporting ministers (now 50 per cent or more of all clergy). For the most active lay people in churches, being a Christian can seem like having two jobs – one paid and the other not. As a local rector I am constantly amazed by the sheer love and generosity of lay people in my churches as they show unselfconsciously that they really know what it is to love the Lord with all their soul and with all their mind and with all their strength – even if their ways of doing so can be a bit strange at times!

It is important for full-time stipendiary clergy to be sensitive to this context in which they follow the sabbath principle and take their time off. I don't mean that ministers should feel guilty about their days off, but rather that they are to be received as a dependable gift of grace and not as a right to be demanded come what may.

There are huge differences of attitude and perception between the two positions. Naomi and Jason found their ministry in their busy suburban church very demanding. They didn't want always to have to go out on her day off to avoid the calls of their parishioners. However, their strategy of pasting a large notice to their front door stating, 'TODAY IS THE VICAR'S DAY OFF. SHE IS NOT AVAILABLE!! CALL ANOTHER TIME!' (yes, it really did say that) caused enormous resentment.

There are lots of ways for clergy to practise the sabbath principle. Dale is nuts about football and is concerned that his church is filled with women and almost empty of men. He joined the pub football club that trains on Thursday evenings and plays matches on Saturday mornings. (The youth section plays on Sunday mornings – he's still thinking about that one!) His weekly day off is Monday. He sees his commitment to the football team as part of his normal ministry and as a little bit of sabbath in the middle of the week.

Denise is an archdeacon. She finds taking a day off every week impossible, so she plans to take three days off as a block once a month. As she is single she is then free to use this time to visit friends and catch up on domestic tasks. She has also joined a Monday evening theatre group that she manages to get to a bit more often than not.

As Don was learning, the sabbath principle is as much a rhythm of grace that you receive as gift from God within yourself as it is a structure of God's time that connects with 'ordinary' time. All time is God's time. Brueggemann's comment that the sabbath shows a 'God who is confident enough to rest' shows that the sabbath rest comes from the heart of who God is. It is not that God, having created time, now must submit to its demanding rhythms in the midst of the kind of busy life that God must lead if the world is somehow to get ordered and blessed. God's gift of time with the sabbath as its sacred centre comes out of his love speaking time and creation into life. That is why the practice of sabbath is as much about what goes on within us, as we learn what it is to trust God and grow in our confidence to rest, as about how we organize our working week. The second is going to be impossible without the first. In reality there will simply be times when this confidence in God's gift of rest can only be received within ourselves when there is a lot going on. Then, when the peak of demand passes, we establish again the rhythm of God's gift of time and rest in our weekly and daily lives.

One problem with all this is that when the demands of ministry are persistently very high and the peak of demand never seems to pass but just goes on and on, the sacred centre of sabbath within God's gift of time can become one more ideal that we just can't hold on to. The call to rest becomes another demand we can't meet. It is all down to us and taking time off is just another d*** thing we have to do. This is one of the painful realities of experience that comes from the distortion of responsibility, relationships and time that we can keep on getting caught up in. We need to be called to see again that the gift of time comes from God as Trinity, love in community. You can't have calling without community. That is why the gift of time, with the rhythms of work and rest, is to be received by people in community with one another rather than by individuals trying to control time by themselves as if we are isolated and solely responsible individuals. We aren't. We need brothers and sisters who love us enough to call us back to healthy rhythms of living where time can be received again as gift not curse.

Fellowship

In Chapter 4 I wrote about fellowship that goes deep enough and far enough to hold us together so that we can grow as the people God has called us to be and go well in the directions God calls us to travel. The quality of the fellowship on offer can literally make the difference between ministry that saps the life out of you and ministry that enables people to thrive even in some of the hardest places. I want to highlight three hallmarks of the kind of fellowship that can make this turn into lived reality. These are fellowship as investment, as gift and as practice.

Fellowship as investment

Fellowship can describe a by-product of church activities: 'Join us for fellowship over a cup of coffee after the service.' Fellowship can be deeply experienced – as in good-quality home groups, cell groups and support groups such as the Jesus Caritas Fraternity I described in Chapter 4. But often what passes for fellowship in churches describes little more than Christians being in the same place at the same time and showing more or less positive regard for each other – from a safe distance.

The New Testament word translated as 'fellowship', *koinonia*, involves generosity and hospitality of heart, hand and home towards strangers as well as to family and friends. *Koinonia* describes the gracious gift of God that bonds Christians to one another in communities of relationship, purpose and hope. *Koinonia* describes people who really belong to one another in the same economy – the economy of God and the economy of life and work that they share.

Koinonia is about people who have a real and far-reaching investment in one another's well-being.

In 1 Corinthians 12, which we visited earlier, Paul describes this investment and interdependency exactly. He says that the level of bonding among members of the body of Christ is such that, 'If one member suffers, all suffer together with it; if one member is honoured, all rejoice together with it' (1 Corinthians 12.26). Here Paul makes the point that the ties – what I have called the investment – that bond people together in the body of Christ create unity out of difference. Earlier, in Galatians 3.27–28, he made this same point for a multicultural setting: 'As many of you as were baptized into Christ have clothed yourselves with Christ. There is no longer Jew or Greek, there is no longer slave or free, there is no longer male and female; for all of you are one in Christ Jesus.' As Paul is writing these letters to people he knew, or at least would come to know in real places in real time, he is setting out foundation principles for Christian relationships, practice and mission. Often it is clear that Paul's letters are replies to earlier letters, not missives out of the blue. He expects the principles he is setting out to be put into action in real places in real time. This level of relationship investment in communities where there are deep differences alongside natural affinities describes a depth of practical *koinonia* that is essential for the well-being and the mission of the people of God.

'Investment' can have unpleasant overtones of self-seeking, even of greed – you invest in something in order to get a profit out of it. Transnational companies 'invest' in two-thirds-world factories, pay the workers a pittance and make enormous profits through high volume and value sales in the West. Certainly we need to be cautious in using this word in relation to Christian fellowship in ministry. But this should not blind us to the reality that fellowship that builds people up and enables them to move forward does involve quality investment of love, presence, attentiveness, time and practical care. Like the message we preach, the fellowship we share is supposed to have real delivery value.

Often the people who come to me make comments along the lines of: 'I sometimes wonder why you think it's worth keeping on bothering with somebody like me.' This may be their insecurity seeking reinforcement and it is important to be cautious, but often it is a real question that goes to the heart of the issues they need to face. We keep on bothering in ministry because people matter to God. This is what Jesus shows us in his 'investment' in humanity and the created world, which has taken him from the fellowship of the Holy Trinity, to the womb of Mary, along the streets of Palestine, through the cross and resurrection to the glory of God in heaven. That's what I mean by fellowship as investment.

Fellowship as gift

When I preach sermons I always find the view from the pulpit fascinating. I see people whose stories, likes and dislikes, hopes and fears, challenges and resentments I know very well; others I don't know so well and new people I still have to get to know. Most of those I see are people I instinctively like; others I have grown to really love; yet others I find difficult at times; and I know that some there find me difficult too. If congregations are communities of difference, that is what you would expect. These are the people I am called to invest in fellowship with in this place at this time. All of them come as gifts from God and fellowship with them comes as a gift from God too.

This is how Jesus describes his disciples in John 17. John's Gospel presents this account of Jesus at prayer as an intimate and holy scene where the Lord is pouring out his concerns to his Father shortly before he crosses the Kidron valley to accept his arrest, trial and death. Four times Jesus refers to his disciples as gifts from God to him – 'those whom you have given me' (17.2, 6, 9, 24). This is very challenging. We know from other parts of the Gospels that Jesus did not always find his disciples easy company and relationships between them weren't always sunny either. These were real people and they experienced real pressures in their relationships with Jesus and each other, but it remains true that Jesus, who has called them his friends, now prays for them as gifts of God to him.

We could be forgiven for wondering what kind of God could possibly give this kind of gift! As the stories I've told so far show, it can be hard at times to see the people we are called to invest our life and work in as gifts from God. Indeed, sometimes the opposite can seem to be more likely. Yet this is part of the challenge we are called to meet. Jesus chooses to speak of his disciples as his friends. Now he prays for them as gifts from God. As Christian disciples we are called to follow Jesus, and this includes the call to speak of those we are called to lead and serve as friends and to treat them also as gifts from God.

We are not, however, called to credulous naivety or baseless idealism any more than Jesus was naive or idealistic. Churches that are open communities will attract all manner of needy, sinful and obtuse people and social misfits – and that's just in the regular congregations! Sometimes clergy feel that the biggest obstacles to the spread of the gospel in their area are the people in the church who claim to be Christians, but who have a visionless perception of what that means. Often they will be right, but they need to be open to God's surprises.

Marion was treasurer of her church council. She was a bitter and angry woman in her late forties who had been widowed through the sudden death of her husband when they were both 22. She rejected any approaches offering care or friendship and was generally experienced as a poisonous and very difficult person. She had attended St James' since childhood. Nobody could remember how she came to be appointed as church treasurer. The vicar thought that she was one of the main reasons his church was not growing, so he prayed long and hard for the Lord to remove her or convert her, preferably the former. Then, during a time of crisis through which a Christian neighbour stuck by her faithfully and refused to give up on her, Marion started at last to pour out her bitterness to God and she came to a renewed faith in Christ. Gradually at first, then more quickly, Marion began to change. She could see the good in other people, went out of her way to welcome them, became the kind of person people want to be with and through whom others also find their way to faith in Christ.

Marion's story is about conversion. Some churches have several 'Marions' – of both genders. Clergy and congregations in local churches are often in major need of conversion if we are to become open, inclusive and authentic in the worship we offer, the fellowship we enjoy, the service we give, the witness we bear. Part of this 'culture of conversion' involves being open to change in the way we see and the way we speak about the people we are called to lead and serve – seeing them as gifts from God, speaking of them first and foremost as friends, investing time, love and patience in their care. Just supposing we made that a ministry priority, what then?

Fellowship as practice

This kind of speaking and seeing does not come naturally or easily. It takes practice to learn how to speak about people in this new way – like learning a new language. Ministers who have become habituated to understanding their ministries primarily in terms of role, task and project management in relation to worship, teaching, fellowship and mission are likely to find this difficult. The 'project management' approach to ministry evaluates people in terms of the contribution they can make or the resistance they represent to the success of the enterprise. It also leads to ways of evaluating our ministries that depend on categories about what we might be able to get out of people. Good people, needy people, quiet people, easily get sidelined. Certainly we are called to be 'wise as serpents and innocent as doves' – tough-minded at the same time as being tender-hearted, as it has been said. What is needed is for us to practise our conversions at the same time as practising our ministries.

To reflect on and talk about

1 What could it take to make you 'confident enough to rest' and wait?
2 What makes the difference between time experienced as gift and time experienced as constraint?
3 How might sabbath time become (re)connected with 'ordinary time' in your and your colleagues' ministry experience?
4 Where do you, or could you, find good-quality fellowship in ministry?

8

Called to be fools

———◆—◆—◆———

I had been going for only two or three minutes and I was bored stiff with my own sermon. The congregation looked glazed, like codfish that had been three days out of the water. I stopped and said, 'This is terrible, isn't it! Shall we sing a hymn instead?' They laughed. We all relaxed. We praised God in song. At the church door after the service one of the men said, 'Funny that, isn't it – you're normally pretty good. Don't worry about it – you can't win 'em all!'

I had a brilliant idea for a family service talk about Jesus being the light of the world and our needing to have Jesus in our hearts if we are to shine out for him. I took a high-powered flashlight and replaced the batteries with banknotes, bits of rubbish and other things that could represent stuff that can get in the way of our relationship with God. I gave a great wind-up about making this powerful torch shine its blinding light in the semi-darkened church, shaking it about when it refused to light up. Then I opened it to find all the junk inside that was getting in the way; and talked about needing the power of Jesus' love in our hearts, while secretly replacing the batteries. Before I switched on again, I asked the congregation, 'What do we need in our hearts if we are to shine as God's lights in the world?' 'Batteries!!' came the resounding reply. Ask a stupid question . . .

I said in Chapter 1 that the right kinds of foolishness have the potential to save us from the wrong kinds of madness in ministry. I want to return to this principle now and take it further by high-lighting two kinds of foolishness that I believe open ways for healing, salvation and renewal in ministry. They are the foolishness of having fun, and the foolishness of Christ. If you are worried that bringing these two together is irreverent, please hang in there and I will try to show why the link can be creative in helping defend us from madness in ministry.

The foolishness of having fun

Writing about fun can be horribly dull! When we try to explain a joke to a friend who didn't find it funny we take the power of laughter away. (Explaining how sacraments 'work' can be like that too.) Most of the stories I have used so far have shown difficulties, frustration, sadness, and the need to refocus who we are, what we are for and what we do. That goes with the territory of this kind of book. In fact I have mostly enjoyed my life in ordained ministry so far. I love being with people 'in all the changing scenes of life', am constantly amazed that God has called me, have an eye for the ridiculous, can't be doing with po-faced religion, and truly believe that there is nothing I would rather spend my life doing. When I preach, people often seem to laugh, though I never write jokes into my sermons. I find having fun in ministry can help restore my balance and bring gospel truth into sharper focus.

Bishop Richard came to the school nativity service in church. As he was putting on his cope and mitre he told me he felt worn out. Then we came into the church, filled with crib, tree, lights, helium balloons, kids dressed as the holy family, shepherds, sheep, wise men, stars, angels . . . and one of the children, beside herself with excitement, called loudly, 'Cor, look at him! It's Dumbledore – he's got his big wizard stick to do magic!' 'Don't be stupid!' said her friend, 'he's a clown – look at his silly clothes and pointy hat!' Richard called out, 'You're both wrong! I'm wearing my dressing-up clothes because it'll soon be Jesus' birthday and we're going to have a party!' The nativity play was then brilliantly done, and Richard picked up the themes of joy, danger, love and giving. He thanked me for inviting him and told me, 'You know, Gordon,

I've been dealing with some tough issues recently. It's great fun being here today – I'm finding it really healing.'

Ministry doesn't have to be fun, but it helps if at least some of it is. This isn't just because it helps us to lighten up and put things into perspective. It reminds us that in the light and shade of the love that calls us we discover some of the shapes of holy joy. Humour that really moves people is often closely related to painful experience. Laughter in the face of what hurts can be cathartic – cleansing. Holy joy isn't necessarily related to having fun or to laughter – both fun and laughter can be self-indulgent and cruel – but it is one of the ways God uses to transform dark and apparently wasteful experiences into resources for healing, blessing and renewal, as we see, for example, in Psalm 85.5–7. As the saying goes, 'joy is love praising; peace is love resting'.

Joy in ministry and the fun that can go with it also helps to fuel the mission of the gospel. Where God's people love one another and have fun together at the same time as being reality-facing, other people are more likely to join them. If I were to propose a strategy for authentic church growth it would be that churches that engage in true prayer and enjoy great parties are likely to grow. The foolishness of holy joy and fun in ministry also shifts our focus from ourselves and our feelings and redirects us towards the love and praise of God. Christians who go round looking like a bulldog that has swallowed a chump chop sideways (to borrow a phrase from P. G. Wodehouse) aren't likely to attract anybody to join them in following Jesus.

One of my first tasks in my present job was to arrange for the closing of our church, built in 1325, for major refurbishment. This work involved taking out all the broken-down furniture that had had its day and recreating the open space of the medieval nave. We decided that we wanted to put creativity, community and church back into the same frame, so we celebrated the reopening not just with special services, but with a vigorous community arts festival that included jazz, folk and classical music, art exhibition, barn dance, circus holiday club, and chat show. People began to catch the vision that the good news of Christ belongs in the same place as celebration, joy, laughter, creativity – as well as in the darker and more shadowy moments of life. Some people think that we are strange and others that we are crazy. Some are uneasy about using the church building for 'secular' things. That's the thing about some kinds of foolishness – it can be taken in different ways that provoke people to wonder.

The foolishness of Christ

I want to look further into the foolishness of Christ using three New Testament passages: part of the Sermon on the Mount in Matthew; Paul's teaching about wisdom and foolishness in 1 Corinthians; and Luke's portrayal of Jesus on the cross.

One interpretation of the Greek word *makarioi*, 'the blessed ones', is that it speaks about those who are held and sustained by the joy of the Lord. The word also carries the sense of those who stand in close relationship with God. The English word 'blessed' has its roots in an Old English expression meaning being 'marked with blood' that relates to conversion to a new faith; and this links with the French *blesser*, 'to wound'. In Matthew 5.1ff. Jesus pictures a reversal of the culture that sees people who are healthy, prosperous and successful as the ones blessed with the good things of life and therefore specially favoured by God. The people Jesus calls blessed are already wounded or vulnerable to being hurt by what life throws at them – the destitute in spirit, the bereaved, the powerless, those who long for the good, the merciful, the pure in heart, the peacemakers and the persecuted – people who have been scarred, bypassed, left out of account or have chosen not to be seduced by the culture of success, self-confidence and personal power. The people described here by Jesus are familiar to any experienced ordained minister. They are people we meet with and pray for practically every day.

What is the 'foolishness' that Jesus brings here to overturn the 'wisdom' of conventional thinking? Anthony Thiselton, commenting on the Sermon on the Mount,[14] says that Jesus sees these wounded and vulnerable people as blessed

> ...because they are driven to abandon self-reliance, to seek the grace of God on God's own terms. Bonhoeffer writes: 'If it is I who say where God will be, I will always find a God who ...corresponds to me, is agreeable to me ...But if it is God who says where God will be ...the place is the cross of Christ' (*Meditating on the Word*, p. 45).

The 'foolishness' of Jesus is that he redefines what it means to be alive to God and to be open to your relations, your neighbours and even your enemies. He does this by calling his disciples to live in the new economy that he calls 'the kingdom of God' – life lived on *God's* terms. This foolishness proposes a counter-intuitive set of priorities. It presents you with a choice. You have to make up your mind. Choosing to go with the foolishness of God in Jesus can provide us with enough sustaining love to keep us ministering in the face of the madnesses that can come with our ministries.

This can lead to experiences that are strange, funny and far-reaching. Once I parked my car outside a cake shop. When I came back the shop owner was smearing a large gateau over my windscreen. He was furious that I had parked outside his shop and he had already covered other parts of my car with cream and custard. My first reaction was anger. For a moment I wanted to punch him in the teeth. Then my Christian instinct kicked in and I realized that God had given me a chance to love somebody who saw me as his enemy. I laughed and asked if I could help him. He looked completely deflated. We sat down and looked together at the mess (it smelled quite nice). He told me that he'd been having problems and my parking there had pushed him over the edge. He asked if I would pray for him and I did. A small and trivial incident like this can help us practise living in the ordinary world with the foolishness of Christ. This can stand us in good stead because when we have to face the big challenges we have some experience of responding to provocation with the love and grace that come from the wisdom of God.

For Paul the ultimate demonstration of God's foolishness is the cross of Jesus. According to Paul, Christ crucified was a real problem for Jews because it stood for complete abandonment by God. So how could it have anything to do with the blessing of God? It was a problem for Gentiles too because they regarded crucifixion as ugly, shameful and disgusting. How could it have anything to do with salvation? But a perspective that is easy to miss, and which Paul brings out clearly, is that the cross of Christ was a problem *even for some Christians*. There is no getting away from it, the cross is a 'scandal' – a stumbling block (1 Corinthians 1.23). In 1 Corinthians Paul is writing to Christians, not arguing directly with non-Christian Gentiles and Jews. He is using the arguments from his mission experience with Jews and Gentiles to call Christians who have already turned to Christ *to return to the cross of Christ*. It seems that some of them *'had tried to move "beyond" the centrality of the cross*, perhaps to a more Spirit-centered, more triumphalist religion'.[15]

The reversal of the world's wisdom that Jesus confronts in his preaching, about who the blessed ones really are, comes to its crisis in the cross. Paul sees this reversal clearly, so he declares bluntly:

> We proclaim Christ crucified, a stumbling-block to Jews and foolishness to Gentiles, but to those who are the called, both Jews and Greeks, Christ the power of God and the wisdom of God. For God's foolishness is wiser than human wisdom, and God's weakness is stronger than human strength.
>
> (1 Corinthians 1.23–25)

Thiselton brilliantly sums up what is going on here:

> Two 'worlds' confront each other at the foot of the cross, with diametrically opposing expectations and claims to 'knowledge'. Illusory or misguided 'knowledge' inflates self-importance

and self-reliance. Appropriation of the affront of the cross brings self-reliance to nothing and turns attention wholly to Christ as the source and channel of effective reality as God reveals it.[16]

All four Gospels say that two other men – criminals or bandits – were crucified with Jesus and that Jesus was in the middle position. This eyewitness detail provides a kind of frame to the picture of Jesus as he suffers and dies. What we see in the frame is supposed to show us some of what it is all for. Matthew and Mark report that these men use some of their last painful breaths to join in the cursing and mocking of Jesus. Luke says that just one of them did this. And he adds something else that he has learned from the people who were there when it happened. One of the criminals seems to see who Jesus really is, struggling there alongside him. He sees himself as he really is too. There's no justice here for Jesus, but he himself is getting what he deserves. He gasps his 'prayer': 'Jesus, remember me when you come into your kingdom' (23.42). Jesus gasps back his promise: 'Truly I tell you, today you will be with me in Paradise' (23.43). Is this criminal's 'prayer' real, or just another bit of sick gallows humour? Who knows? God knows because God was there, and God receives this person with Jesus either way.

None of the Gospels tells us directly what the cross of Christ 'means', except in the stories and sayings that surround it. From a distance it looks just like any other set of crucifixions. It doesn't mean anything more than a few more condemned men nailed up. Close up we see hellish injustice, violence, cruelty, cynicism, love tearing apart – and a whole lot more. Yet Christians say that the crucifixion of Jesus of Nazareth is the starting point of 'salvation'. After the cross of Jesus there is nothing in human sin, suffering or alienation that lies beyond the furthest reaches of the saving, healing love of God. Jesus' cross shows that there is nowhere God won't go 'to seek out and to save the lost' (Luke 19.10). If anything, Paul is understating it when he calls

'Christ crucified . . . the power of God and the wisdom of God'
(1 Corinthians 1.23, 24).

How extraordinary, then, that it is surprisingly easy for Christian
clergy to exercise ministries that are generally about God and goodness, drawing on Jesus' teaching and compassion and encouraging
people to live Jesus' way, while allowing the cross of Jesus to drift
slowly away into the background. The cross *is* degrading, disgusting, utterly foul, because it is Jesus – God with us – who hangs
there suffering and dying in radical solidarity with the condemned
criminals struggling for breath next to him. He 'who knew no
sin' dies bearing their and everybody else's sin. It *is* hard to stay
with if you allow yourself to see what is really going on there. The
soldiers and bystanders had seen it all before – here were three
more nobodies being crucified. But that's the point. At the cross
of Jesus, God declares that nobodies matter enough to die for.
The cross is just ugliness, foolishness and waste for people who
can't or won't make the connection between the suffering of Jesus,
the love of God and the need of the world. There is nothing
beautiful or good to be found there. But for those who can and
do make the connection, however falteringly, this is the starting
point for the wisdom of God to begin regrowing beauty in the
lives of men and women – the gateway of 'salvation'.

If we allow the foolishness of the cross to recede into the background of our ministries, we put ourselves in danger of building
salvation out and building madness in. Look for a moment at the
titles of our first seven chapters, and take them to the base of the
cross. Who you belong with, where you are going, what makes you
holy, what makes you human, who you serve, how you lead, where
you find ultimate rest and final peace, all find their identity, purpose
and meaning here. I saw a picture in Strasbourg of St Bruno in
front of the cross of Christ. At first I thought that Bruno is turned
half away from the cross because he can hardly bear to look. Then
I looked again. On the beam above Jesus' right arm sits a small bird
singing. Bruno seems to be listening intently to both the cross and
the music of the new creation being announced from it.

Of course, the cross is not enough. The cross is the power of God and the wisdom of God because of the resurrection. The first disciples didn't go out preaching about Jesus just because he was crucified, however wonderful they thought he was. They went because he rose from the dead, they had met him, talked with him, eaten with him, been blessed by him, and received the Holy Spirit as he promised. They went out with the good news because they couldn't stay in with it. There is no space here for an extended reflection on the resurrection, so I will just focus on two texts, one from the New Testament, the other from a Church Father.

Paul ends his reflection on the resurrection in 1 Corinthians 15 with: 'Thanks be to God, who gives us the victory through our Lord Jesus Christ. Therefore, my beloved, be steadfast, immovable, always excelling in the work of the Lord, because you know that in the Lord your labour is not in vain.' The resurrection is the reason that there is work to do and the source of the grace and strength to do it.

John Chrysostom's 'Paschal Homily for Easter' captures the passionate liveliness of the risen Lord. Here is part of it:[17]

When he descended into hell, he plundered it . . .
[Death] was dismayed because it was trampled on; it was in
   bitterness
Because it was deceived.
It had taken hold of a body and was confronted by God.
It had taken hold of the visible and the invisible had routed it,
Death, where is thy sting? Where, hell, thy victory?
Christ is risen and thou art brought to nothing.
Christ is risen and the devils are fallen.
Christ is risen and the angels rejoice.
Christ is risen and life has prevailed.
Christ is risen, and the dead are delivered from the grave.

Our ministries are to be focused and energized by the cross and resurrection of Jesus and the values and commitments that come out of that. If we simply minister general kindness by emphasizing the presence of Jesus who is alive and for people because of the resurrection we are taking a seriously wrong turning and leading other people in the same direction. No cross → no resurrection → no salvation → no ministry that has anything Christianly distinctive to offer. This is putting it bluntly. Certainly we need to interpret what makes for 'salvation', but always this interpretation will be energized by this particular kind of foolishness of God.

You would expect ministry that follows the foolishness of Jesus in the way of the cross and lives in the light of the resurrection to lead you into some dark places and to hold some surprises, and it does. The calling to be 'fools for the sake of Christ' may lead to our not only being sometimes out of joint with the social cultures we live among, but even being dissidents in relation to our own churches.

St Hilary's (Hilly's) is a church with a distinguished record of sponsoring peace and justice issues. It serves two sharply contrasting social areas. On the hilltop around the church itself are large detached houses in substantial grounds separated from each other by parkland where people jog, play football and walk their dogs. This is where about a quarter of the parish population live and where most of the regular worshippers used to come from, the rest travelling in from well-heeled communities nearby. At the bottom of the hill, a few hundred metres away to the east, and accessible to the church only by a steep pathway and a gateway through a retaining wall, live the remaining three-quarters of the parishioners, many from eastern Europe, in mid-rise apartment blocks. Since Josh moved to Hilly's with his family two years ago, he has set himself the task of visiting as many of his parishioners as possible wherever he can meet them. He quickly learned that there were no shops in the lower part of Hilly's parish. He got some grant money together and rented two empty flats as a coffee drop-in with a food bank, nearly new clothes store, and advice centre. Some volunteer members of the congregation were pleased to help staff these as part of their Christian service.

After some months, families from the flats began to ask Josh to baptize their children. Although they mostly came from Orthodox and Catholic backgrounds, they were moved by the love and commitment he showed them and had started to regard him as their priest. After a further year, people from the flats began to come to the services at Hilly's in some numbers – soon they made up over a third of the regular congregation. Some of the church leaders came to Josh privately and told him that they thought he should start a special church plant down in the flats where 'the immigrants' would be more at home, and it would save them having to toil up the hill. Josh considered this, but said that he thought the gospel would be served best by building up Hilly's as a multicultural church where people of difference could worship together and recognize each other as 'all one in Christ Jesus'.

A few weeks later, none of the people from the flats came to the morning service. After the service Josh walked down the path to the gateway in the wall and found that it had been blocked up so solidly that nobody could have got through it without crowbars and hammers. He asked the church leaders who had spoken to him about their church plant idea if they knew anything about it. One of them said, 'The people from down there don't belong up here. It would be better for them to have their own church down there. It makes no sense for them to drag their old people and their kids up that hill.' One of them admitted that he and some of his friends had blocked the gateway. He told Josh, 'There's nothing you can do about it now. It would take a sledgehammer to shift that lot. What's done is done.' Josh thanked them for being honest with him, then told them that their attitudes and actions were profoundly unchristian and they must start getting some gospel priorities straight – and they could start by unblocking the gateway. Then he went home, rampaged around his study with the door shut, tried to pray, couldn't sit still, stand up, or lie down. He considered resigning and going somewhere else. He felt crucified by his pain with people who were proud to sponsor social justice issues but wanted to shun the poor on their own doorsteps.

He knew that Jesus wanted to bring resurrection to all this, but felt that it was hard to believe this or do anything about it. He phoned a group of ministry colleagues and asked if they could meet with him to talk and pray . . .

St John's is next door to the town hall and is often used for big civic services. Since Gavin came as rector nine months ago he has made no secret of his passionate commitment to pacifism. At the Remembrance Sunday service, attended as usual by large numbers of soldiers and civic dignitaries, Gavin chose to wear a white poppy on his robes instead of a red one to demonstrate his commitment to pacifism. He preached a message about Jesus' commitment to non-violence, and military action always being a result of political failure. He pushed his argument further by asking the congregation whether by wearing red poppies they were just going along with the culture, rather than allowing themselves to think critically about it. At the church door the congregation left without greeting him. Next day he was the front-page story in the local paper and the lead on the radio news.

One Sunday morning I preached a sermon about forgiveness based on Matthew 18.21. The next day Marge called me to complain about what another church member had said to her. She told the story of her offence at great length and with considerable passion. Eventually she said, 'Well, Gordon, what do you have to say to that?' I took a deep breath and reminded her of what I had been saying about forgiveness in yesterday's sermon. She shouted at me, 'Do you mean to tell me that I'm supposed to forgive that ****** woman?' I said that the only way for Christians to sort out hard stuff between them does include the need for forgiveness and reconciliation. 'Well, I've never heard anything so disgusting in my life!' she said, then put the phone down.

These three stories give examples of dissidence at work within local church ministry. Josh found himself at odds with his established church members over their attitudes to 'the strangers within your gates'; Gavin wanted to take a firm stand against the 'celebration of warfare' and used his white poppy and his privileged position as the preacher to do this; faced with Marge's bitter anger, I wanted to press home my message about forgiveness. However, it would be short-sighted to assume that the three of us here have any automatic claim to the moral high ground in these stories. Being a dissident is no guarantee of being right, and is likely to put you in the firing line – from your own side, as well as from other angles.

It is true that Josh had been able to recruit a few people from his church to help staff the drop-in at the flats. Could he have helped his settled church people to respond more positively to the newcomers if he had taken more care to listen and talk and pray with them, to teach them about God's priorities for the poor and to include them in more of his ministry down the hill? Maybe he assumed that given this church's track record on social justice issues it would not be a problem. But the issue of social and cultural inclusiveness of people of difference within the body of Christ *in that place* would not go away. It would still have to be faced. The question here is what it would have taken for this church to face it together – and in the meantime you have to respond positively to the people who are here with you now. Josh sought the advice and support of his bishop and of his cell group prayer partners, and gained renewal of grace and love to hang on in there and keep ministering to all parts of his parish.

Gavin's confrontational approach served to offend and alienate everybody in his community – even more so in light of the fact that a soldier from his parish (a former choir member) had been among the earliest of those killed on active service in Afghanistan. Gavin had not taken the time to listen to and learn from the people he was called to serve. They felt that he had abused his position and even done violence to what they were there to remember and give thanks for. He claimed afterwards that he had spoken from the heart and with real openness about his convictions. This was true but it was not his only calling at that service. And his defensiveness showed that he was still not listening. If he had taken time to join his own church, and listen and learn, he may have gained the respect of the people, who might have listened and learned in return from what he wanted to say, in less high-profile contexts, about non-violence and the ethics of military service.

I think that I responded too quickly to Marge's bitterness by pressing her to apply the message about forgiveness before she was ready and able to hear it. Perhaps if I had been able to stay longer with her anger, we might have been able to find the real sources of her pain and open them to God's love and grace so that forgiveness could become a real possibility, not an insulting accusation. Perhaps.

Dissidence in ordained ministry is not always, or even very often, focused in dramatic events like these. If we preach and teach faithfully from the Bible what the call to follow Christ together involves, our message is bound to rub up against people's commitments, attitudes and problems. A simple way to explore this is to read between the lines of some parts of the New Testament letters. For example, Colossians 3.12ff. promotes the values of compassion, kindness, meekness, patience, forgiveness, love, peace, thankfulness and the indwelling word of Christ. If these are reversed you get something like harshness, unkindness, arrogance, impatience, resentment, hatred, disturbance, ingratitude and Christ's word being left aside. This is admittedly a crude and polarizing exercise, but it can serve to help us reflect on what evidence there is among us to back up the oft-repeated claim that Christians are somehow different (and better) because we have come to Christ and our lives have been changed. We live in the context of public cultures that (alongside a whole lot that is very good) fuel promotion of the values of narcissism, competitiveness, cruelty, contempt and blame. In relation to this, Christians who 'have been raised with Christ [are to] seek the things that are above, where Christ is' (Colossians 3.1).

We are called to be fools for Christ's sake, but it is not our aim to be identified as subversive dissidents. This may happen as a consequence of faithful ministry, but that is not our main purpose.

However, I have said enough to show that if we minister with gospel integrity we are likely to find the experience uncomfortable for at least some of the time. The distress caused by our fellow Christians can be enormous, sustained and debilitating (often more so in my experience than stress caused by non-Christians). As we come towards the end of this chapter I want to suggest two resources that can help us sustain ministry without madness. These come from our discipleship as Christians and from the discipline of our ministries. Most of this book has been about the need for ministers to allow our identities and actions to be strengthened through becoming more and more open to the gospel that we ourselves preach, so I won't labour the point. We are ordained lay people and in relation to the people we serve and lead we are fellow disciples of Jesus Christ.

Discipline in ministry is about the commitment to live and work together in the community of God's people. This community gets its focus in the life of the local church, but is bigger than the local parish. In the Church of England the definition of the local church is not the parish church in a particular place, but the churches in a diocese that share in the mission and ministry of their bishop. The structures that serve as the framework for our life and work together are provided by the bishop's licence or commission, the networks of ministry relationships, church law (canon law), ministry development review and accountability processes, and public law. Ministers of most 'independent' churches serve within frameworks of disciplined ministry relationships, accountability, and public law. It is true that some people find church structures stifling, but I don't think they need to.

Church of England clergy are licensed to our ministries by our bishops. This makes all the resources of our diocese and national Church available to us, along with giving us a clear range of ministry, mission and pastoral care responsibilities. The freedom we have to arrange our working lives is something many other working people would envy. We have professional advice – liturgical, educational, vocational, technical, legal and a whole lot else – available free of charge for the asking. There are people responsible for overseeing our ministries and who are committed (in principle at least) to our care and welfare. There is certainly a lot about the structures (mostly, but not always, the people who deliver them) that could be improved, but taken as a whole the disciplines and structures within which ordained ministers work are intended to be the frameworks for freedom.

In my work as a diocesan training officer I was asked to look at a deanery (an area group of churches) where half of the dozen or so clergy were off sick with stress at the same time. Was this an unfortunate coincidence of neighbouring people experiencing misfortune, or was there something more systemic that needed attention? As I visited all the clergy in the area, I discovered that they had a number of complaints, including that they felt isolated in their ministries; they had difficulty getting holiday cover; the area they were working in was unusually difficult (it was); they had little sense of fellowship and trust between them; and they didn't see how the diocese could help, so they had to manage on their own. Between them they had a culture of being 'hard done by' – even of victimhood. All these clergy lived within four miles of each other, but they hadn't sought each other's help 'because all the others are over-busy too'. The resources of the diocese were available to them, but they didn't feel confident about accessing them. Several complained about the inadequate church structures that made their ministries so difficult.

It seemed clear to me that the isolation these clergy were experiencing (and it was certainly real enough) was far more attitudinal than structural. This did not lead me to think that they all needed to pull themselves together, trust each other more, pool resources, and ask the diocese for help. Their problems were real. In any case, you can't produce good-quality fellowship in ministry, that promotes healthy relationships and shares resources, just by flicking a switch or compiling a report. My thinking was that these good but struggling brothers and sisters needed renewal in their Christian discipleship and relationships. They needed to be called again to their vocations in Christ and in their ministries. They needed the healing in ministry that comes from knowing that you are respected, and loved, such that when you seek help and support this will be a sign of health, not of weakness. They needed the kindness, encouragement and practical help, not only to be on offer *but to be delivered*, if they were to make the transition from seeing themselves as victims of their vocations to being agents in their ministries. A key delivery system for this could be provided by the disciplines and structures of vocation and ministry that had been left unused.

Discipleship, discipline and direction belong together in ordained ministry. Without the lively, curious and surprising discipleship of following Jesus Christ, the disciplines of ministry and the structures of the Church are utterly tedious and completely pointless. Clergy who have ceased to follow Jesus – or who still follow him, but at a wary distance – cannot lead other people in the Christian way, although they can and do sometimes run 'successful' churches. Without discipline, discipleship is a sham that can slide into disillusion, eccentricity and futility. 'Discipline' here carries two related meanings: the framework structures that give shape and direction to our ministries, and the committed seeking, finding and following of Jesus in the company of brothers and sisters who will help us to know the truth that makes you free. A Morning Prayer collect expresses this combination of discipline and discipleship vividly: 'O God, the author of peace and lover of concord, to know you is eternal life, to serve you is perfect freedom.'[18]

Nobody can be a disciple alone. Discipline without community is nonsense. Discipleship describes who you follow, where that is leading you and who you are travelling with. Discipline does the same things at the same time as providing shape, structure, legitimacy and direction in ministry. If Christian ministers are called to be fully engaged 'fools for the sake of Christ' in ways that can make us sometimes lovingly out of joint with the values of our society and the practices of our churches, we need the security of knowing what kind of covenant we are supposed to be living in. Without that, the way lies open for all sorts of madnesses to develop in our ministries.

To reflect on and think about

1 'The right kinds of foolishness have the potential to save us from the wrong kinds of madness.' What possibilities and what problems does this idea set up in your imagination?

2 What questions does Paul's call for *Christians* to return to the foolishness of the cross raise for you and your colleagues in ministry?

3 Why do you think established Christians often find the gospel of Christ foolish, or even offensive?

4 Where might we find the spiritual and emotional resources to live ministries that are both 'in place' and 'out of joint' in our churches and the communities we serve?

Epilogue

Mystery

One

One of the most maddening things about working with God is that he insists on using grace rather than power as his main ministry strategy. In fact God seems to delight in working around the edges of things rather than just guiding us in answer to our prayers, setting the direction we should go and travelling companionably to bless us on our journey. God's insistence on grace is what makes for mystery in ministry. By mystery I don't mean confusion. In Christian theology 'mystery' means something that is hidden at the moment, but will be revealed in God's good time. Seeing the work of clergy as 'mystery' means that it is here to be discovered rather than there to be constructed, to be glimpsed rather than grasped. Certainly we need to minister from the best knowledge and with the best skills and the deepest commitment we can bring – that's what loving God 'with all your heart, and with all your soul, and with all your mind, and with all your strength' (Mark 12.30) means. God's grace does not absolve us from poorly conceived and carelessly delivered ministry. Well-constructed ministry without grace might build churches, but it won't make Christians who can witness to their faith. In reality it doesn't work quite as neatly as that because we tend to stumble about in the way of Christ rather than always striding out after him. I think that about a fortnight after we get to heaven, it will all be clear.

If I'm honest I would say that quite a lot of the time in my ministry I really don't know as clearly as I would like to what is going on and what I'm supposed to be doing. I used to worry myself sick about this before I began to realize that the grace of God is first to be received, then to be lived, then to be preached – in that order. Because we want to be effective in our ministries we try to use our time as effectively as possible, and this can lead to our filling our diaries with meetings and stuff because we can't cope with the spaces. My personal view is what I call the 40/60 law of ordained ministry. For 40 per cent of the time we have a reasonable chance of being clear what we are doing – for example, saying our prayers, reading Scripture, preparing for or leading worship, leading or taking part in planning meetings, consultations. For the other 60 per cent of the time we aren't so clear – we are faced with all manner of opportunities, encounters, challenges, choices. Many of us say that we need more space, but we are anxious about what we will do with it, so we find it very easy to build it out of our diaries so that the unclear proportion gets minimized. If we are very busy, we have little time to think and it can make us *feel* useful and important. But most often it is in the spaces where God walks 'in the cool of the day' and calls out, 'Where are you?' that we find ourselves living our ministries most truly.

I was in a tearing hurry between meetings and rushed into a shop to buy a sandwich to eat on the way. A young man stopped me. He looked as if he'd been crying. I thought he might have been drinking. 'Are you a vicar then?' he said. I muttered assent as I was mentally, if not actually, backing away from him. 'Can you say a prayer for my dad, cos he's just been told he's got cancer?' I said that I would, hoping that I could remember to. 'No,' he said, 'I mean, can you say a prayer for him now?' So I prayed with him, then rushed off to my meeting. A week later I was in the shop buying a newspaper and the same man was there. 'Hello, Vicar,' he said. 'Thanks for your prayers. There must be something in it, mustn't there? I mean, Dad's a lot calmer and more peaceful now.' Grace – there must be something in it.

Laura says that her vocation to ordained ministry came to her through something I said in a sermon I preached at her church. I often preach from a full script and I did so then. I know that I didn't say what she says she heard, but it is clear that God spoke powerfully to her while I was preaching that evening. Many of my fellow clergy can tell stories of God working with them, around them, through them, in ways that are off-centre to us. I take such moments of grace to be signs of his love that calls us to ministry without madness.

Two

What happens if we do experience 'madness' in the course of our ministries? Even people who trust in grace and allow themselves to live out of the foolishness of God in Christ can be at risk of falling into sin, running into danger, becoming mentally unwell and emotionally exhausted under the pressures of ministry. In any case, we are human. We share with everybody else the risks of becoming sick, and we can fail in our ministries, just as other people can have problems in their walk of life. So we need to have at least the start of an answer to what should happen next. I have written enough to show that I believe our mission is to live the gospel we preach. This means that if we sin we are called to repent; if we get lost we need to be found; if we become sick we need healing; if we are lonely we need companionship and care.

I was present at a bishop's staff meeting one day when the discussion was about a priest who was struggling and nobody quite knew what to do with him. Somebody said that perhaps he should be taken out of ministry altogether. Bishop Michael said firmly that before this was even considered we should be clear about what redemption might look like for this man, and we should explore all avenues that could lead to redemption. We must ask what Christ might want to bring out of this dark and difficult situation. This is vital if we really believe that 'the Son of Man came to seek out and to save the lost'.

The most difficult step is to admit to ourselves that we have a problem, and we need help because we can't handle it on our own. This may be clear to our families or to other people long before it is obvious to us. The Church – as institution, as well as in the form of local reconciling community – needs to be a safe enough environment for people to be able to face tough personal realities and engage with them. That is really what this book is all about. Once we ask for help, the resources to deliver what we need can be opened up. Sometimes these are in the form of provision by agencies such as medical care, confidential counselling, psychotherapy, TLC (often the most effective), discerning prayer ministry, spiritual accompaniment. Sometimes what is needed is simply extended time off to recover our energy and our sense of proportion; or a place of retreat and care where we can experience a 'kind holding' while we discover afresh that 'the Lord is here: God's Spirit is with us'. The aim is to restore us to our full humanity in Christ, and enable us to return to our present ministry or take the first steps in finding a new direction.

It is fair to say that not all the resources on offer are at their best all of the time. It would be naive to say that those who care for the Church's ministers get it right every time, but in my own experience the resources available to support Church of England ministers and our families are often very good indeed. The stories I have told here include examples of parish ministers and senior clergy who have wondered what they are about, who have lost their way, or have even experienced burnout and breakdown. Most of these stories have positive outcomes, not because I like to have happy endings, but because in the face of the struggles that ministry often delivers, my experience is that God's grace in combination with practical human love can be powerfully healing. At the end of it all, it is the foolish grace of God in Jesus that makes for ministry with fruitfulness and without madness.

Resources that can help when you need them

Even when you are doing all the right things, living your faith in Christ as you minister, the pressures can build up. The following are a few representative examples of the resources that can be helpful.

Building up a network of good friends and colleagues with whom you can be real and truthful about how things are for you is essential. Isolation and loneliness are the hardest things to bear when ministry is at its toughest.

Church of England Dioceses, Methodist Districts, and other Christian Churches in the UK have lists of counsellors to whom clergy can self-refer for fully or part-funded absolutely confidential help. Often the first six sessions are free and the fees are negotiable after then. Access to information about these is via diocesan and other church websites and clergy handbooks. To maintain client confidentiality, no personal records of referrals are kept and no reports are made.

Christian centres specializing in ministries of health and healing and pastoral care can be great places for 'being held', resting and renewal. Often their resources include first-class hospitality, skilled listening, spiritual direction and prayer ministry. In themselves or in combination with professional counselling and psychotherapy, they can be a safe and potent resource for renewal, refocusing and refreshment in ministry.

- Burrswood, Groombridge, Tunbridge Wells, Kent TN3 9PY <www.burrswood.org.uk>. BACP accredited counselling also available.
- Crowhurst Christian Healing Centre, The Old Rectory, Crowhurst, Battle, East Sussex TN33 9AD <www.crowhursthealing.co.uk>.

- The Society of Martha and Mary, Dunsford, Exeter EX6 7LE <www.sheldon.uk.com>. Provides special resources of hospitality, with the availability of counselling, massage, and prayer specifically designed with needs of clergy and other Christian ministers and their families in mind.

For a comprehensive list, contact The Retreat Association <www.retreats.org.uk>.

Notes

---

1 Arnold van Gennep, *Les Rites de passage/The Rites of Passage* (Paris: Sorbonne, 1909; London: Routledge, 1960).

2 David Augsburger, *Dissident Discipleship: A Spirituality of Self-Surrender, Love of God, and Love of Neighbor* (Grand Rapids: Brazos Press, 2006).

3 Henri J. M. Nouwen, *The Return of the Prodigal Son* (London: Darton, Longman and Todd, 1992), p. 90.

4 Yvonne Warren, *The Cracked Pot: The State of Today's Anglican Parish Clergy* (Stowmarket: Kevin Mayhew Ltd, 2002), p. 76.

5 Eucharistic Prayer A, *Common Worship: Services and Prayers for the Church of England* (London: Church House Publishing, 2000), p. 185.

6 Rowan Williams and Joan Chittister OSB, *For All That Has Been, Thanks: Growing a Sense of Gratitude* (Norwich: Canterbury Press, 2010), pp. 66, 73.

7 Stanley Hauerwas, *Hannah's Child: A Theologian's Memoir* (London: SCM Press, 2010).

8 *The Alternative Service Book 1980*, p. 357.

9 A very fine exception is Justin Lewis-Anthony, *If You Meet George Herbert on the Road, Kill Him* (London: Mowbray/Continuum, 2009).

10 Raymond E. Brown, *The Gospel According to John*, Vol. 2 (London: Geoffrey Chapman, 1972), p. 682.

11 See <www.churchleadershipfoundation.org>.

12 Gerhard von Rad, *Genesis* (London, SCM Press, 1961), p. 62.

13 Walter Brueggemann, *Genesis, Interpretation Bible Commentary* (Atlanta: John Knox Press, 1982), p. 35 (emphasis added).

14 Anthony C. Thiselton, *1 Corinthians: A Shorter Exegetical and Pastoral Commentary* (Grand Rapids: Eerdmans, 2006), p. 45.

15 Thiselton, *1 Corinthians*, p. 44 (italics in original).

16 Thiselton, *1 Corinthians*, p. 45.

17 Olivier Clement, *The Roots of Christian Mysticism* (London: New City, 1994), p. 54.

18 *Common Worship: Daily Prayer* (London: Church House Publishing, 2005), p. 166.

Printed in Great Britain
by Amazon

48839224R00102